A Friendly Guide to THE OLD TESTAMENT

MARIE TURNER

Published in Australia by
Garratt Publishing
32 Glenvale Crescent
Mulgrave, Vic. 3170

www.garrattpublishing.com.au

Copyright © Marie Turner 2014

All rights reserved. Except as provided by the Australian copyright law, no part of this book may be reproduced in any way without permission in writing from the publisher.

Design by Lynne Muir

Images: www.thinkstock.com, Lynne Muir

Scripture quotations are drawn from the New Revised Standard Version of the Bible, copyright © 1989 by the Division of Christian Education of the National Council of the Churches of Christ in the USA. Used by permission.

All rights reserved.

Nihil Obstat: Monsignor Greg Bennet MA (Oxon), LSS, D.Theol
Diocesan Censor

Imprimatur: Archbishop Denis Hart DD
Archbishop of Melbourne
Date: 21 September 2013

The Nihil Obstat and Imprimatur are official declarations that a book or pamphlet is free of doctrinal or moral error. No implication is contained therein that those who have granted the Nihil Obstat and Imprimatur agree with the contents, opinions or statements expressed. They do not necessarily signify that the work is approved as a basic text for catechetical instruction.

9781921946974

Cataloguing in Publication information for this title is available from the National Library of Australia.
www.nla.gov.au

Every effort has been made to trace the original source of copyright material contained in this book. The publisher would be pleased to hear from copyright holders to rectify any errors or omissions.

CONTENTS

FOREWORD 3

INTRODUCTION 4

WHAT IS THE OLD TESTAMENT? 6

HOW THE OLD TESTAMENT CAME TO BE 8

HISTORY 11

THE BOOKS OF THE OLD TESTAMENT 18

THE HISTORICAL BOOKS 30

THE PROPHETS 36

THE POETRY:
PSALMS, WISDOM AND APOCALYPTIC 39

THE WISDOM BOOKS 42

APOCALYPTIC WRITING 45

GLOSSARY 48

FOREWORD

For many people, the Old Testament is both fascinating and overwhelming. This Friendly Guide hopes to introduce first time readers, or readers who have little experience of the Old Testament, to these ancient texts. The Old Testament is much longer than the New Testament. This Friendly Guide does not attempt to cover every book; it takes a selection of texts from the various divisions of the Old Testament and offers a way of reading them that will help them "come alive" for the contemporary reader.

In the Jewish Bible the Old Testament is organised into three categories: the Law, the Prophets and the Writings. In the Christian Old Testament the books are divided into the Pentateuch, the Historical Books, the Prophets and the Poetry and Wisdom books. This Guide will give an overview of these divisions, and will select some from each category to treat with more depth.

It is not well-known among beginning readers that the different Christian traditions name a slightly different collection of books as their sacred Scriptures. For example, the Protestant traditions have thirty-nine books in their Old Testament, but the Roman Catholic tradition has forty-six books. The reason for the difference has its origins in the history of Israel, and the spread of its peoples into areas of the ancient world beyond Israel. In the section entitled "What is the Old Testament", a brief history of Israel is given to show how this situation came about. A short foray into the formation of the canon will help to explain how various church communities came to recognise these writings as the "word of God".

Since the books of the Old Testament come from a wide range of periods and contexts, the historical events and figures selected for coverage are those which best serve for an understanding of the biblical texts.

The Friendly Guide then offers some insights into representative texts from the various divisions of the Old Testament. The treatment will necessarily be brief, but it is our hope that the pages you are about to read will whet your appetite for a life-long exploration.

[11] Wisdom teaches her children and gives help to those who seek her. [12] Whoever loves her loves life, and those who seek her from early morning are filled with joy.
(SIRACH 4: 11–12)

INTRODUCTION

I have spent many years reading, pondering, and teaching the Old Testament. It may seem strange that someone should spend a large part of a lifetime learning and teaching about one section of one book: the Bible; but—of course—both the Bible and the Old Testament are not *just one book*. They are made up of many books. I never get tired of these books, and if I spend the rest of my life learning and teaching about them, I will never cease to be excited by them. That is because the Old Testament is a rich kaleidoscope of images of God, of characters who loved that God, and of the events that shaped their stories and beliefs about God.

In this Friendly Guide I will be able to explore with you only a part of the Old Testament. If you have your Bible open in front of you, or if you take it to your room each night to read before sleep, or if you have ever been a bit puzzled by some of the readings you might have heard during a Sunday Liturgy, you might find it a bit overwhelming. Indeed, if you are already quite familiar with it, you might still find it difficult in parts. That is because we are dealing with ancient texts written in a culture and time far removed from our own.

Yet these books have stood the test of time. They are sacred books for people of the Judaeo-Christian traditions, but they are also appreciated by many non-believers because so many of the books of the Bible have inspired great writers and playwrights to draw upon them for inspiration. Most of the plots in the great literary classics were first found in the Old Testament: the first murder of a brother by a brother because of jealousy; the great love stories of Ruth and Naomi, of David and Bathsheba; the refusal of people to be bound by the chains of slavery. You are perhaps already familiar with the many modern songs which have their basis in the words of the Old Testament books. The Rock group U2 always used to finish their concerts with an adaptation of Psalm 40; you may have seen the musical, *Joseph and his Amazing Technicolour Coat*; you may remember the Byrds' song, 'Turn, turn, turn'; and is there anyone who can keep still when 'By the rivers of Babylon' gets airplay?

All of these have their basis in the words and stories of the people of the Old Testament. Many of our proverbs come out of the Old Testament. Have you ever cautioned someone by saying: "Fools rush in where angels fear to tread?" It comes from the book of Proverbs. An old song uses a proverb for its opening line, "Wise men say only fools rush in..."

In this Friendly Guide you will meet these wise men and some of the wise women too! One particularly fascinating "wise woman" is the figure of Sophia. Readers who meet her in the great wisdom poems will be left

Bergamo: Moses crossing the Red Sea

wondering, "Who is she? How did she emerge from these ancient Jewish texts?" Interwoven with all these stories and themes is the perennial question: who is this God of Israel?

At various times the people we meet in the Old Testament have loved, responded to, cried out to, and even rejected their God. At times they turned to other gods; but in the final analysis, they returned to the one God who had been with them from the beginning. The Old Testament is indeed a love story. Some theologies emphasise the distance between God and human beings; in the pages of the Old Testament you will encounter a God who loves the people with a passion, and who hopes that the love will be returned. Sometimes it is, and sometimes it isn't. And that is the core of the Old Testament, and the reason its pages are full of such drama.

No matter how often or how deeply we read these ancient texts, they never fully give up their secrets. They always beckon us to re-embark on another journey to find previously undiscovered pathways. I hope this Friendly Guide to these ancient and sometimes "unfriendly" stories will help you as you begin or continue your own exciting and lifelong path of discovery.

WHAT IS THE OLD TESTAMENT?

The Hebrew Bible is divided into three sections called the Law, the Prophets and the Writings. In Hebrew, the language most of the Old Testament was written in, these sections are called the *Torah*, the *Neviim*, and the *Kethuvim*. When we take the first letters of each of these sections they form the word, TaNaK, and this is what Jewish people call their bible. They do not use the term Old Testament because it presumes the New Testament which, of course, Jewish people do not include among their sacred Scriptures.

The Hebrew Bible and the Old Testament are not quite the same thing. The books of the Hebrew Bible are set out in a different order from the Christian Old Testament. Even the Old Testament is different for the various Christian denominations. The Protestant tradition recognises thirty-nine books as their Old Testament, while Roman Catholics, Orthodox, and Eastern Rite Catholics have more. Roman Catholics have forty-six books in their Old Testament; they call these additional books the deutero-canonical books, meaning the "second canon", while the Protestant tradition refers to them as "apocryphal" books.

STRUCTURE OF THE OLD TESTAMENT

Hebrew Bible	Christian Old Testament
TaNaK: an acronym for the three divisions	**Pentateuch** Genesis, Exodus, Leviticus, Numbers, Deuteronomy
Torah (The Law) Genesis, Exodus, Leviticus, Numbers, Deuteronomy	**Historical Books** Joshua, Judges, Ruth, I and II Samuel, I and II Kings, Ezra, Nehemiah, I and II Chronicles
Nevi'im (Prophets) Former: Joshua, Judges, I and II Samuel, I and II Kings, Ezra, Nehemiah, I and II Chronicles Latter: Isaiah, Jeremiah, Ezekiel, The Twelve (Hosea, Joel, Amos, Obadiah, Jonah, Micah, Nahum, Habbakuk, Zephaniah, Haggai, Zechariah, Malachi)	**Poetry and Wisdom** Psalms, Job, Proverbs, Qoheleth (Ecclesiastes), Song of Songs, Esther, Lamentations In addition, in the Roman Catholic tradition: *Deuterocanonical Books (Apocrypha)* I and II Maccabees, Sirach (Ecclesiasticus), Wisdom of Solomon, Judith, Tobit, Baruch, Additions to Daniel, Additions to Esther
Kethuvim (The Writings) Psalms, Job, Proverbs, Qoheleth (Ecclesiastes), Ruth, Song of Songs, Daniel, Esther, Lamentations, Ezra-Nehemiah, I and II Chronicles	**Prophets** Three Major: Isaiah, Jeremiah, Ezekiel Thirteen Minor: Hosea, Joel, Amos, Obadiah, Jonah, Micah, Nahum, Habbakuk, Zephaniah, Haggai, Zechariah, Malachi, Daniel
39 BOOKS	**46 BOOKS** Eastern Rite and Orthodox traditions have all the above books plus others.

Before we look at the books and their arrangement in our various sacred Scriptures we need to go back in time to the ancient world so that we can understand how these differences have come about. Today, English is probably the most widely-spoken language; wherever we travel, we will often find someone who understands English or speaks it a little, even in some of the more exotic parts of the world. In a similar way, in the ancient world, Greek was widely-spoken and understood. Some of the Old Testament books were written in Greek and others were translated into Greek from the Hebrew. These Greek translations became known as the Septuagint. It was the Septuagint version of the Bible that Roman Catholics adopted as their sacred Scriptures.

How the Old Testament Came to Be

The whole process of the compilation of the books of the Hebrew Bible and the Old Testament was rather complicated. The story begins in the wonderful, ancient city of Alexandria. This is not the place where the Scriptures were first written, but it is the city where the Greek translation that we know as the Septuagint was undertaken. It is this translation which forms the basis of the Roman Catholic canon of Scripture.

Alexandria and the Septuagint

In Israel, the people spoke Aramaic, a Semitic language common in the Ancient Near East. The written language of the Bible was mainly Hebrew. However, since the time of Alexander the Great (356–323 BCE), the main language of the ancient world was Greek. As the Jewish people were exiled by various conquerors at different times, or emigrated by choice to regions outside Israel, they adopted the local language. When they could no longer read Hebrew, the Jewish people of "the diaspora" or "dispersion" needed translations of their Hebrew Scriptures into Greek.

One of the chief centres for the Jews of the Diaspora was Alexandria in Egypt. Alexandria is known for the famous Pharos Lighthouse, one of the seven wonders of the ancient world. But the city in its heyday was also known as a glorious intellectual centre.

Alexander the Great is considered to be the founder of Alexandria in 332 BC, but archaeological evidence attests to building constructions dating seven hundred years earlier than Alexander's invasion of Egypt. Its cultural significance stretches over a period of about one thousand years before it started to decline. In its earliest three centuries it was perhaps the leading cultural centre of the world, with architecture that could compete with Rome and

Pharos lighthouse, Alexandria, Egypt

Athens. Its population was one of different religions and philosophical orientations. It was also an important trading post because it supplied an overland connection between the Mediterranean and Red Seas.

The Library

Alexandria was also famous for its Royal library, founded during the reign of Ptolemy II. In the third century BCE it had five hundred thousand scrolls, and was at one time the largest library in the world. The *Musaeum*, a centre of research with laboratories and observatories, was part of the complex. Scientists and scholars of various disciplines would visit the library from all over the ancient world to study. Scholars who visited included Archimedes, Euclid and Ptolemy. Often, scientists would re-write old scrolls that were badly written or growing brittle with age.

The Septuagint

From this intellectual milieu emerged the Greek Bible, known to biblical scholars today as the Septuagint (also written as LXX). The Septuagint derives its name from a legend. *Septuaginta* is the Latin word for seventy. When it was decided that the Torah needed to be translated into Greek, seventy of the top Greek and Hebrew-speaking scholars were assigned separate rooms in Alexandria, and at the end of seventy days they emerged with exactly the same translation! However that may be, it was a highly respected translation.

At first, the term Septuagint was used to refer only to the translation of the Pentateuch; but then other biblical books were translated into Greek and included. Eventually, books such as the Wisdom of Solomon—which was written originally in Greek in Alexandria—were also included.

Throughout the centuries, there has not been agreement as to the actual books the Christian Churches would consider to be their Scriptures. Eventually, all the Christian traditions agreed on the same twenty-seven books of the New Testament, but the situation is different with the Old Testament. The Protestant canon uses the Hebrew Scriptures as the basis for their canon—the list of books they consider to be their Scriptures. This is known as the Masoretic Text (MT) and was compiled in the early Middle Ages by a family of Jewish scholars known as the Masoretes.

The Roman Catholic and Orthodox traditions use the Septuagint books as the basis of their canon. The manuscript translation behind both the MT and the LXX is very complex. Because a text is written in Hebrew does not necessarily make it older than the Greek translation. There are some very old manuscripts behind the Greek.

Augustine preferred the more extensive Alexandrian canon while Jerome preferred the narrower Hebrew canon. The Catholic Council of Trent (1546) accepted the wider

Above: Alexander the Great
Below: Bibliotheca Alexandrina

Did You Know?

The library was probably destroyed by fire, but to this day the details of the destruction remain somewhat of a mystery. However it was destroyed, it was a great loss to humanity. In 2003, the Bibliotheca Alexandrina was inaugurated near the site of the old library.

Some examples of the manuscripts scholars work with are illustrated below. You can also appreciate, perhaps, the beauty of Hebrew script.

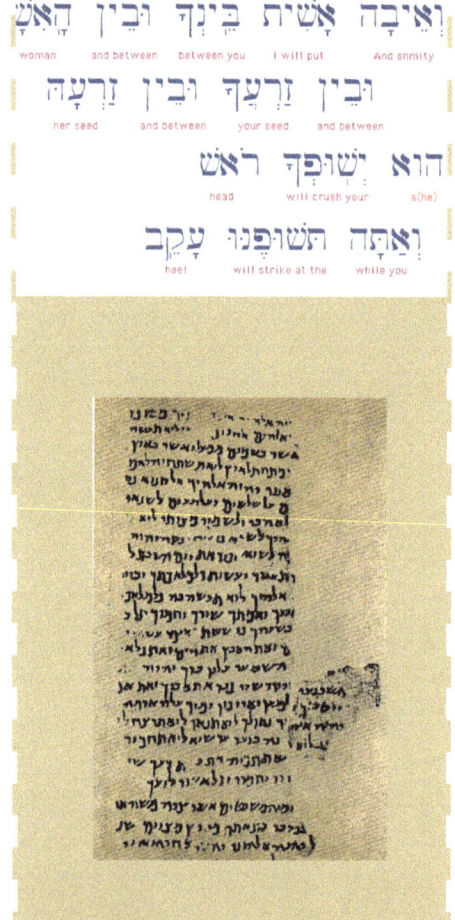

Alexandrian (Greek) canon on the grounds that it contained books that had been used by Christian communities from antiquity. Thus, for the Roman Catholic, Eastern and Orthodox traditions, the issue was decided not on whether particular translations were older, but on whether the church community had always used the books as Scripture.

Most New Testament writers, including Paul, quote the Bible according to the Septuagint (Greek) when they refer to the Old Testament Scriptures. Of course, the New Testament writers do not call it the Old Testament, but simply "the Scriptures". Jesus and his earliest Palestinian disciples probably used the Hebrew Scriptures, as that would have been the natural language for them to use.

Modern textual scholars of both Catholic and Protestant traditions work together now to offer the best translations based on good manuscripts. As you can imagine, issues of the canon of Scripture and the various translations provide a lifetime of research for Textual Critics!

A diagram might help to clarify the relationship between the Greek and Hebrew manuscripts:

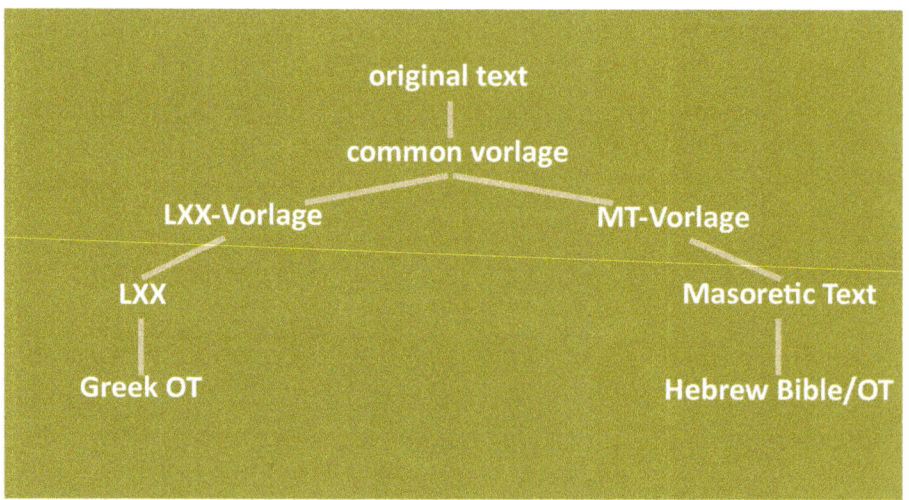

'Vorlage' is a word referring to a previous or original version of a text—sometimes lost to us—that a new text has been based on.

Did You Know?

Modern English translations of the Bible are based on the printed editions of the Hebrew Bible and the principal ancient Latin and Greek translations. In turn, these printed editions are based on ancient manuscripts. In the case of the Hebrew Bible, the most important manuscripts date from the tenth and eleventh centuries CE; so the manuscripts behind the Hebrew Bible, upon which our English translations are based, date from approximately a thousand years after the Jewish canon was fixed. The text found in these manuscripts is known as the Masoretic Text (MT), dating from the Middle Ages.

HISTORY

Israel was a small country surrounded by powerful nations. The four main powers whose course of history affected Israel were Egypt, Assyria, Babylonia and Greece. It is not quite accurate to speak of these as countries, or to think of them as affecting Israel in separate, identifiable time periods. They were an ever-present reality in the history of Israel, but these nations also had their periods when their fortunes waxed or waned, when they were more or less powerful.

Because of this, they were at various times more or less threatening to Israel. They were also a source of influence on Israel in terms of culture, education and even religious belief. In spite of all this, Israel developed its own unique culture and religion. Alone among the ancient peoples, Israel developed early on a monotheistic faith, that is: a belief in the one God. Because the name of this God—Yahweh—is held in such reverence by Jewish people, traditional Jews do not pronounce the name. Out of respect for that tradition, I will use the "tetragrammaton", which is the letters that the Hebrew uses for the name—YHWH—and will write them in capital letters.

ISRAEL

The earliest Hebrews were semi-nomadic. Stories about Abraham and Sarah and their descendants are set too far back in time for us to be sure how historical they are. They are usually referred to as the Ancestor Narratives, or the Patriarchal Narratives, because they tell of the earliest named ancestors of the Jewish people. The most

Abraham

famous of them, Abraham, is also considered the faith ancestor of both Christian and Islamic peoples; he is the forerunner of those of us who are believers in the three great monotheistic faiths: Judaism, Christianity and Islam.

It is unlikely that Abraham and Sarah were themselves monotheists, but they probably had a belief in a patron god who would protect their clan. In later developments, the descendants of Abraham came to believe in one God; for the most part this God was called YHWH or Elohim.

The story of Abraham, which begins in Genesis 11:26, gives us some fascinating insights into the roads which these nomads took in their wanderings. Although these accounts are often told in the form of legends, they give us some historical insights that, in general, are confirmed by archaeological discoveries. This is not to say that we can read the stories as history in the modern sense, but we can get an idea of their lifestyle.

According to the tradition recounted in Genesis 11:28–31, the ancestral home of Abraham was the southern Sumerian city of Ur, in present-day Iraq. Genesis 11:31 tells us that Abraham's family settled in Haran in northern Mesopotamia, a region in present-day Turkey, near the Syrian border. It was there that Abraham obeyed God's call to set out on the wanderings which led him to Canaan, on to Egypt, and then back to Canaan where he died and was buried.

A well-known biblical verse connects Abraham with Aram, a term which refers to Paddan-Aram (the region where Haran was located): "A wandering Aramean was my ancestor; he went down into Egypt and lived there as an alien, few in number, and there he became a great nation, mighty and populous."(Deuteronomy 26:5) This short verse tells in a nutshell the early history of the biblical peoples and their nomadic wanderings!

The World of the Ancient Hebrews

Eventually, these wandering nomads moved down to Egypt. Genesis 12:1–10 recounts the journey of Abraham and Sarah through Canaan, down towards the Negev, and eventually into Egypt, because of a famine in the lands they were travelling through:

> [8] From there he moved on to the hill country on the east of Bethel, and pitched his tent, with Bethel on the west and Aï on the east; and there he built an altar to the LORD and invoked the name of the LORD. [9] And Abram journeyed on by stages toward The Negeb. [10] Now there was a famine in the land. So Abram went down to Egypt to reside there as an alien, for the famine was severe in the land.
> (GENESIS 12:8–10)

From Genesis 12:1–10, we can get an idea of the nomadic lifestyle of the early Hebrews. Perhaps you can imagine them sitting around the camp fires in the evening, remembering and retelling the clan stories and reciting their genealogies. Genealogy is a thread that runs through the Book of Genesis. It was especially important in an oral-aural culture, and preserved the family histories and connections.

The people of Canaan were not all nomadic. Freshwater springs attracted nomadic peoples and more settled societies around the area of Jericho for centuries. Archaeological discoveries have shown that 10 000 years ago there was a permanent settlement in Jericho of small round or oval houses, partly sunken, with walls made of mud-brick. In the Neolithic Age there were stone fortifications, house floors and walls were plastered and polished. Clay figurines have been found. Animals were domesticated, crops were cultivated and trade with neighbouring peoples was carried out. If you recall the story of Joshua and the Battle of Jericho, it is clear that there was already a stone-fortified city at Jericho. These are the walls which "came tumbling down", according to the biblical account of the battle in Joshua 6. The town of *Ras Shamra* on the Mediterranean coast dates back to 7000 BCE.

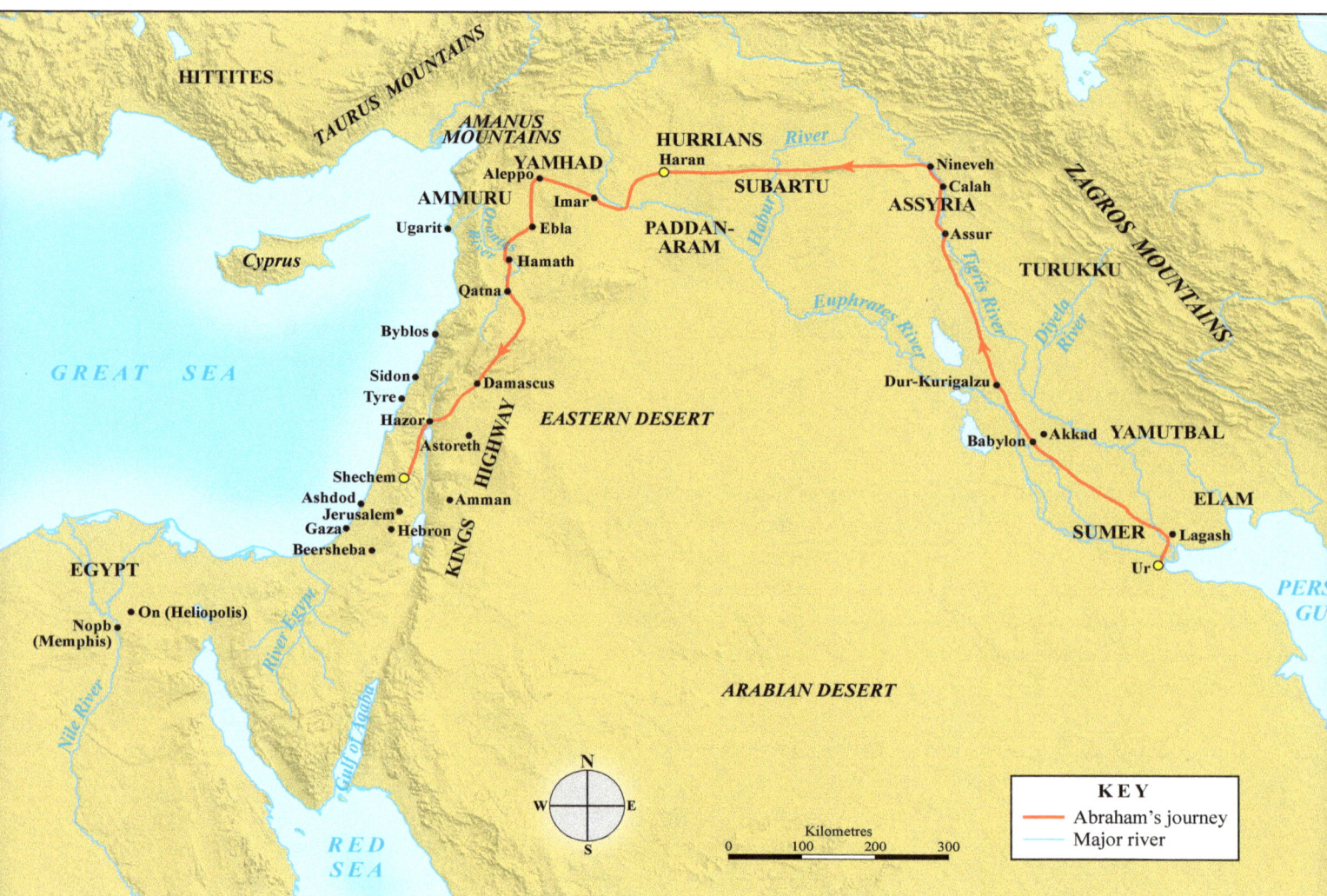

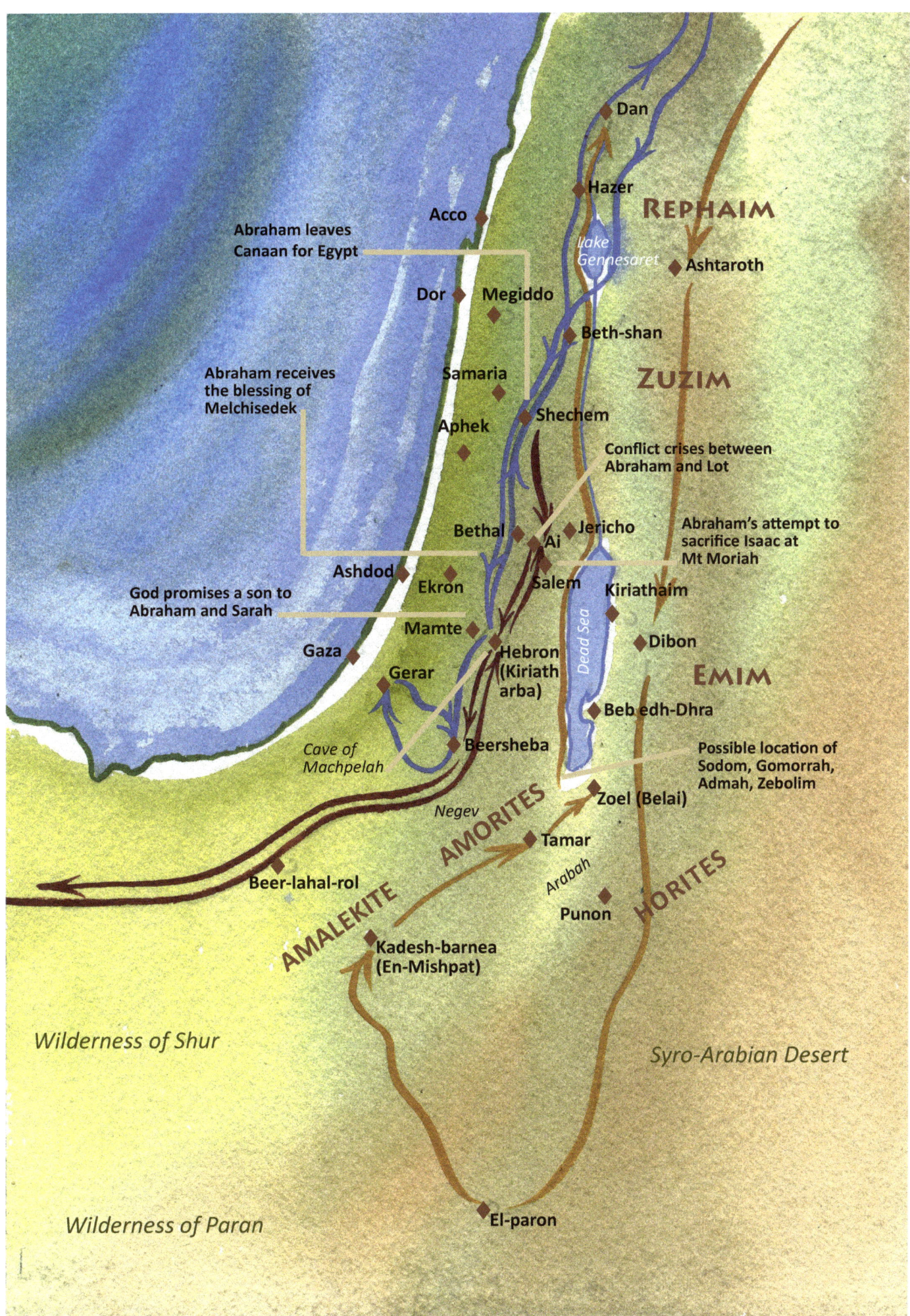

Statue head of Ramses II at Ramesseum, Thebes, Egypt

Egyptian Art Depicts its Gods and Goddesses: Horus with Isis and Seti

ANCIENT EGYPTIAN/HEBREW TIMELINE

2000–1800	Egyptian control: Middle Kingdom
1800–1700	Abraham, Sarah and descendants (Genesis)
1700–1550	Asian Hyksos control
	Descent of Jacob's family into Egypt
1600–1400	Egyptian control
1400–1300	Amarna Age (An age of Egyptian weakness)
	• Akhenaton (1370–1353): New Kingdom
	• Tutenkhamen (1353–1344)
1300–1200	Egyptian revival (Exodus, c. 1290)
	• Ramses II (1290–1224): probably the Pharaoh depicted in the Book of Exodus
	• c. 1250–1200 Israelite conquest of Canaan (Book of Joshua)
c. 1170	Ramses III defeats Sea Peoples
	Late Dynastic Period
from 1000	Period of decline
	Libyan Dynasties
715–663	Nubian Dynasties
671–652	Assyrian Rule
663	Thebes sacked
609–593	Neco II of Egypt defeats Josiah of Judah at Battle of Megiddo

Egypt

It is not surprising that the nomadic lifestyle of Abraham and Sarah took them to Egypt. Egypt was a major power in the area and controlled Canaan long before the Hebrews settled there. In Egypt there are still early villages waiting to be discovered under the Nile mud. Along the Nile Delta, archaeologists have discovered oval wickerwork dwellings, the remains of pottery and some copper ornaments. Egypt reached the peak of its power under the Ramessids (19th Dynasty) and then steadily declined. It is probable that the era depicted in the Abraham-Sarah narratives was around the second millenium BCE.

A time-line of the history looks like this: (See left panel)

You may be familiar with the musical, *Joseph and his Amazing Technicolor Coat*. You may even now start singing "Any dream will do"! This is a contemporary musical interpretation of the journey of Joseph (Abraham's descendant) into Egypt; followed later by his father (Jacob) and his brothers: the forerunners of the Twelve Tribes of Israel. (See map)

Assyria

Another neighbouring power which featured largely in Israel's history was Assyria. You may have heard the poem which begins, "The Assyrian came down like the wolf on the fold" (George Lord Byron, *The Destruction of Sennacherib*, 1815). Assyria lay to the north and its capital was Nineveh. In the books of prophets such as Micah, you will hear about the Fall of Samaria to Sennacherib. Samaria was the chief city in the north of Israel which fell to the Assyrians in 722–21 BCE. Assyrian power

expanded during the ninth century BCE. After the capture of Samaria, Assyria declined rapidly. It was defeated by Egypt in 660 BCE and Nineveh, the capital, was captured by Babylon in 612 BCE.

BABYLONIA

Babylonia had one of the most far-reaching impacts on Israel even to this day and, deriving from Jewish history, the history of Christianity. It is hard to believe that an event which took place in the fifth century BCE could still

Babylon was supreme in the eighteenth century BCE under Hammurabi. The "Code of Hammurabi" (circa. 1772 BCE) is the law code which influenced law codes such as the Ten Commandments. For a time, Babylon became subject to Assyria, but was all powerful again after 625 BCE. Babylon under Nebuchadnezzar captured Jerusalem in 597 BCE. In 587 BCE Nebuchadnezzar beseiged Jerusalem and this time the city was destroyed, the Temple fell and large scale deportations to Babylon

Ancient Persian ruins

affect us today, but that is what happened with the defeat of Israel at the hands of the Babylonians and the exile of the Israelites to Babylon in 587 BCE. It was in Babylon that much of the Bible took shape and Judaism as we know it had its formative experiences.

You may find it hard to keep from tapping your feet when you hear the song, 'By the rivers of Babylon'. It is a good tune to dance to, but a tragic event lies behind it.

took place. The scattering of Jews from their homeland is known as the Diaspora (dispersion). Those who were exiled were the political, ecclesiastical and intellectual leaders of the Jews. They lived in special settlements near Babylon and they were not harshly treated. Opportunity for economic advancement persuaded many of them to remain in Babylonia even after Cyrus' Edict allowed their return to Judah.

PERSIA AND THE RETURN OF THE EXILES

The Persians destroyed Babylon in 538 BCE, which began the Persian Period. Persia was a great power from the time of Cyrus (550–529 BCE). Cyrus proved to be an enlightened ruler. He respected his subjects' beliefs and allowed cultic autonomy. He allowed those who had been deported by the Babylonians to return to their homelands. In 538 he issued an Edict allowing the return of Jewish captives to Judah and provided funds for the rebuilding of the Temple.

Very few of the exiles returned to their homeland, which was referred to by the Persians as the Province Beyond the River and Judea, the land of the yehudim. It is from this Hebrew word that we derive the word "Jew".

One of first tasks of those who returned was to restore the altar of holocausts and re-establish a regular cultic worship. In 537 the foundations of the Second Temple were laid. Those who had remained in Judah and had not been taken into exile did not welcome the returned exiles. Nor did the returned exiles welcome the help that the Samaritans offered to rebuild the Temple. They did not trust the Samaritans who had intermarried with neighbouring peoples and had been infiltrated with other religious groups after the Fall of Samaria in 721. Opposition between the Jews and Samaritans hardened. We see an example of the outcome of this rivalry in the dialogue between Jesus and the Samaritan woman in Chapter 4 of John's Gospel.

Between 538 and 522, a further group of exiles returned under the Governor Zerubbabel and the High Priest Joshua, and the Temple rebuilding intensified. During the Feast of the Passover of 515, the Second Temple was dedicated.

Little is known of the situation in the next half-century, but during this time the province of Judah was set up with the Northern limit at Bethel and the Southern border a little below Bethlehem. In the west, Judah was bounded by the province of Ashdod. The full restoration of the Jewish community was left to the Priest Ezra and the Governor Nehemiah (See the Books of Ezra-Nehemiah). Judah was now organized as part of the Trans-Euphrates satrapy of the Persian Empire. Until the rise of Alexander the Great, the history of Judah is closely tied to the history of the Persian Empire.

The Hellenistic Period

Persia was conquered by Alexander the Great of Macedonia in 330 BCE which ushered in the Hellenistic Age. Alexander conquered Israel in 333 BCE. After Alexander's death his generals were dominant in Israel in turn:
- The Ptolemies (Lagids) of Egypt (320–198)
- The Seleucids of Antioch in Syria from 198–63 BCE.

Pompey the Roman General triumphed over the Seleucids in 63 BCE. From this time, Israel was under Roman rule. The Roman General Titus captured Jerusalem in 70 CE. The Siege and Fall of the Second Temple was a watershed in Jewish history that has repercussions to the present time. The Temple has never been rebuilt and conflict in the Middle East ensures that Jerusalem and the site of the ancient Temple remains a source of division to this day.

Biblical History

The importance of knowing the historical setting for an understanding of the Bible will become apparent when we realise that the time period the books describe and the time of their final writing as we have it in our Bibles did not usually coincide. Events as they happened were often recounted orally and later came to be written down in an edited

Arch of Titus, Forum Romanum, Rome

fashion, within the framework of the religious convictions of Israel. To our modern minds, history should try to observe and record events as objectively as possible, while at the same time we acknowledge history is always selective and interpreted by historians. Biblical history, however, works on different premises. There was not the same understanding of cause and effect. To our mind, one country becomes powerful, its interests are threatened in some way by another power, and then diplomacy or war comes into practice. To the ancient biblical mind, God was at the centre of the cause-effect mindset. If Israel was invaded and its people taken into exile, it was because Israel had not been faithful to its covenant with God. The most influential historians of the bible to expound this conviction were a group we refer to as the Deuteronomic historians. These historians worked from the perspective of the Exile in Babylon. How could a faithful God allow the covenanted people to lose so much and suffer so much? The books of the Bible from Joshua through to II Kings are the Deuteronomic historians' "take" on Israel's history and how Israel came to be in exile.

The time of the exile in Babylon was a time of intellectual activity as the writers sought to preserve their traditions for future generations by committing their beliefs, history and traditions to writing. The first book of the Bible is Genesis and it was precisely in the exile in Babylon that Genesis was compiled. But the oral traditions of creation had been told for centuries before they came to be written as we know them in our Bible.

The Books of the Old Testament

Genesis

Although the book of Genesis is not the oldest biblical book, there are good reasons for starting our exploration of the Old Testament there. The final editors of the Old Testament clearly wanted to begin by witnessing to their belief in God as their creator. Later they would show how God was also their liberator from oppression, but at the beginning they wanted to reflect on their origins. The book of Genesis can be divided up in the following way: (See below)

If you have ever read the story of creation in the book of Genesis closely, you may have been struck by the differences and apparent contradictions in the first two chapters of the book. For example, in Genesis 1:26 God makes humankind on the sixth day; but in Chapter Two of Genesis, God creates the man, first because otherwise there would be no one to look after the garden God was about to create (Gen 2:5–7). There are other differences in Chapters One and Two, but the creation of humankind is the most noticeable. These should not be considered contradictions, however, when we realise that there are at least two different writers at work in these chapters and they each have their own story of creation to tell.

The creation narratives were told orally in many forms before they were written down in the forms we now have them in the Bible. The Hebrew people heard stories in their surrounding cultures but adapted them and re-told them in ways that expressed their belief in the one God who created everything. The writers were working with their own contemporary knowledge of the world. We are dealing here with primeval history, i.e., pre-history rather than history. Its purpose was to create meaning in reference to the profound, essential questions of human existence and to express this meaning through myth. When we use the word "myth" in reference to the Bible, we are not using it in the popular, everyday understanding of it. When we use it in the context of sacred Scripture,

A. Genesis 1–11
These Chapters tell the story of the origins of the world and humankind. They cover:
the Primeval event–creation, flood, the tower of Babel and the scattering of peoples throughout the earth.

B. Genesis 12–50
These chapters tell the story of the origins of the nation of Israel. They cover:
Abraham and Sarah and their descendants:
Abraham, Sarah and the Egyptian wife of Abraham, Hagar: chapters 11–25
Descendants of Abraham and Sarah: chapters 26–36
Joseph "novella": chapters 37–50
Israelites in Egypt: Joseph powerful in the court of Pharaoh
The Joseph narrative sets the scene for the book of Exodus and slavery in Egypt:
"Now a new king arose over Egypt who did not know Joseph." (Ex 1:8)

Genealogies occur throughout Genesis
The genealogies are an important (if dull!) literary theme symbolising the spread of humankind according to God's command in Genesis 1:22: "Be fruitful and multiply."

it has a very particular sense. The usual understanding of "myth" is a story, similar to a folktale, using traditional themes and motifs which tell tales of human relationships to the gods. Myth in this conventional sense often refers to ancient beliefs of a polytheistic nature in cultures where the people believed in several gods. These are not precisely the kind of myths we mean when speaking of "myth" in the Bible. A biblical myth is a story that seeks to express profound truths about the relationship between God and humankind and indeed the whole of created existence. There are many questions about human existence that are universal, that is, they are questions that people of all times and places share. In contemporary society we prefer our accounts of creation to be scientific, but we need to acknowledge that was not the intent of the biblical writers.

When biblical scholars ponder the Genesis narratives, and indeed all the biblical texts, one of the questions they begin by asking is "What form of literature are we reading?" This question is helpful, because it identifies the particular conventions of the form so that we have a better understanding of what the original author was trying to convey. As an illustration, we might think about contemporary literary forms. Whenever we read any form of literature, we have to keep in mind the conventions of that form. We do not read historical fiction or science fiction in the same way we read history or science. We expect different things of these forms. Sometimes we analyse poetry and other times we just immerse ourselves in its images and rhythms. We read historical fiction and history quite differently. We expect a good writer of historical fiction to research well the pertinent time period; we expect them to present as accurate a picture as they can of the characters they are writing about; but we also expect them to draw upon their imagination to construct an interesting and informative story that will make the time "come alive" for us.

God creating Adam

When we read a history text book, however, we expect more "objective facts". When we understand and respect these conventions we are much more in tune with the author's meaning. Another example might be email messages and a more formal letter. Email messages are brief and to the point and are usually composed quickly and answered promptly, whereas a more formal letter, be it a business letter or a personal one, is written in a more carefully constructed way. We know what to expect from each.

When we seek to understand the meaning of an ancient text such as a biblical text, it is very important to understand the form of writing the ancient author was employing. Biblical scholars call this "Form Criticism". To ignore this aspect of the biblical text might result in serious misunderstanding of the author's meaning. It would also be an abuse of the text if we seek to make it conform to something the original author never intended.

Some forms of literature we encounter in the Bible include the following:

Myth: for example, the creation narratives reflecting some mythological features

History: for example, some of the court history in the books of Samuel may be based on the Annals of the Kings of Judah and Israel

Legends, sagas and folk history

Call Narratives (for example, where a prophet is called by God or Jesus calls his disciples)

Law Codes

Proverbs, many of which survive to the present day in common usage

Prophetic literature

When we read the Bible we should always ask ourselves what form of literature the original author was using to spread his or her message, and we should read it accordingly to the best of our ability. That becomes a significant issue when we read the creation narratives of the book of Genesis. We should not expect these books to conform to modern scientific knowledge. The original writers certainly would never have heard of the Big Bang or Evolutionary Theory. The purpose of these books was not to teach us about science but about the Creator God. They had quite a different world view from ours. For example, if they were to construct a diagram of the ancient cosmos it might look something like this:

> [5] The LORD saw that the wickedness of humankind was great in the earth, and that every inclination of the thoughts of their hearts was only evil continually. [6] And the LORD was sorry that he had made humankind on the earth, and it grieved him to his heart.
> (GENESIS 6:5–6)

Creation narratives are common to all races throughout the world. The biblical writers inherited the traditions and shaped them into their own literary narrative and theological belief.

WHO WROTE THE BOOKS?

We refer to the authors of material in the Pentateuch as "sources". The two most important sources are the Priestly Source for which we use the letter "P" and the Yahwist source for which we use the letter "J" (due to it first being labelled this way in German).

THE PRIESTLY SOURCE (P)

The first account of creation in the Bible comes from P, the "Priestly" writer who was particularly interested in the objects of cultic worship. The material comes from the sixth century BCE during the period of the Babylonian exile. It was probably written down in Babylon.

Gen 1:1–2:4a, which we assign to P, has a schematic construction of six days of creation, followed by the Sabbath rest. Fundamentalist readers of the Bible seek to argue sometimes that God created the world in six days, or at least a set time period symbolised by six days. This type of interpretation

Behind the creation texts are oral traditions and pre-history that reflect the fact that Israel was united with its surrounding world. Behind the texts can be traced a history of creation motifs from early Sumerian through Babylonian and Assyrian right down to the later Greek versions. There is a common history of reflection on creation stretching over thousands of years right through to the present. Creation narratives are common to all races throughout the world: They attest to the desire for humankind to reflect upon the realities of the world they inhabit and the presence and actions of God in that world.

The biblical creation narratives have parallels in the Ancient Near Eastern texts of the Babylonian and Canaanite creation myths:

- Gilgamesh Epic
- Enuma Elish
- Atrahasis story

The Atrahasis story displays the same basic plot as Gen 2–9:

Creation of Human Race

Problems with the Human Race:
- Noise of multiplied human race bothers Enlil

Flood:
- Enki is ordered to flood the earth
- Atrahasis is ordered to build a boat
- Earth is flooded
- Aftermath

Gods suffers hunger and thirst when sacrifices cease

Yet it is clear that the Bible has adapted this basic story to tell it in the framework of one God. In the polytheistic myth, the gods destroy earth because they cannot stand the noise made by human beings; in the Bible account, God floods the earth because of the moral fault of humanity:

STRUCTURE A

When we divide the text up in this way we can see that P thinks of God's act of creation as bringing order out of the chaotic "nothingness", as it were. God separates:

Darkness	from	Light
The Waters Above	from	The Waters Below
The Land	from	The Sea

The verses can be divided thus:

1:1–10	Creation of living space
1:11–25	Creation of life
1:26–31	Creation of humankind in image of God and summary of creation
2:1–3	Rest and Sabbath
2:4a	These are the generations… (note the use of the genealogy idea)

STRUCTURE B

Another structure we might discern is this one:

Days of Creation

1 Light	4 Luminaries
2 Waters/Firmament	5 Fish/Birds
3 Dry land/Vegetation	6 Land animals/People
Day Seven:	**God Rests**

quite misses the crucial motif of the Sabbath rest, which was so important to the exiles when they were far removed from their Temple worship. The exiles sought to base their observance of the Sabbath in the original (eschatological) Rest of God.

The P writer uses the name "Elohim" for God until Chapter Three of the book of Exodus when God's name is revealed to Moses as *YHWH*.

To help us with an overview of Genesis 1:1–2:4a, it is useful to think of the way P constructed his narrative. Biblical scholars call this kind of methodology "Literary Criticism". There are a couple of alternative structures we might focus upon. (See above)

For P, creation culminates in the Sabbath Rest: God "rested" on the seventh day. P's interest in the Sabbath reflects the importance this writer places on the regulations of worship.

In the Image of God

The climax of created life is humankind—male and female—in the image of God. The human beings are to have dominion over all the living creatures of the Earth and to subdue them. The Hebrew word for "subdue" used in this verse is "*radah*". If you say it aloud, you can sense its harsh sound. No matter how much the word is watered down because of contemporary environmental concerns, it remains a problematic word for modern ears. The word must be understood in the context of the whole verse: "Be fruitful and multiply, and fill the earth and subdue it; and have dominion over the fish of the sea and over the birds of the air and over every living thing that moves upon the earth."

The verse has connotations of vitality and an abundance of life: according to God's command, there will be teeming life upon earth. Seen in this context, the command to have dominion and subdue the earth reflects the idea conveyed in the Genesis passage that humans were to rule the earth in the manner of an ancient Oriental ruler with the responsibility to be in control and ensure order in his domain. It is difficult for contemporary readers to understand this mindset, but if we consider that for the ancient people nature could be seen as threatening and something to be kept at bay, it makes some kind of sense. It is a text which reminds us that we need to face the challenges of some of the biblical texts and acknowledge that they emerged from a culture and life-experience quite different from our own. Our task is then to adapt the concepts we find challenging and transform their meaning for a contemporary situation. Biblical scholars call this process of adapting the ancient sense for a new context "hermeneutics".

This perplexing verse alerts us to the idea that P understood humans as the earthly agents of the heavenly ruler, God. According to Genesis 1:26–27, God created humankind, male and female, in God's own image. The creature, adam, is made male and female in the image of God: "in the image of God he created it, male and female he created them." Readers of the Bible often ponder how it is that human beings are "made in the image of God". It is a profound verse but quite confusing if we try to work out how we as bodily mortals can be like the eternal, transcendent God. The verses are not so much saying something about the nature of humankind; rather, they are saying something about the relationship between God and humankind. "Created in the image and likeness of God" means God has established a relationship between God and humankind. Humanity as a whole

has been created as a counterpart of God. One of the crucial values inherent in this text which may resonate with contemporary readers is that this concept of all humanity in relationship with God holds true despite any differences among people. No religion, or belief, or place, or culture is excluded. All humanity has been created in the image and likeness of God and is thus already in relationship with God.

P's account is a poetic celebration of the God whose powerful word brings creation into being. The creative act is simply put: *"God said ... And it was so"* (Gen 1:3–4, 6–7, 9, 11, 14–15, 24, 26). It is God's word which brings creation into being. The mysterious wind of Genesis 1:2 that sweeps over the face of the water could also be God's spirit. The Hebrew word is the *"ruah"*, which is the word for spirit or wind. It is the creative power of God that brings the order out of chaos (the deep). At the completion of creation, God's verdict is positive: "God saw everything that he had made, and indeed, it was very good." (Gen 1:31)

YAHWIST SOURCE (J)

The designation "J" which we give to the writer of Genesis 2:4a–3:25, the "Adam and Eve" narrative, comes from the German word for YHWH (Jahveh) because the Yahwist uses the name YHWH for God. The German is used because it was German scholars who first brought to our attention the different sources in the Pentateuch (the first five books of the Bible). Jewish people substitute for Yahweh the word "Adonai" meaning Lord, out of reverence for the sacred name.

The J material which we have in Genesis dates from the tenth century BCE and may have originated in King Solomon's Court. The narrative is full of anthropomorphisms, that is, it depicts God as a human being. For example, although the writer knew that God was spirit, he shows God walking in the garden of Eden in the cool of the evening, God has nostrils from which the breath of life comes and God plants a garden. The Yahwist uses literary motifs that were familiar in the folklore of the surrounding ancient cultures, e.g., the tree of life, a cunning serpent and so on. We find the Yahwist at work in the second creation narrative in Genesis 2:4b–3:25.

The narrative of Genesis 2–3 might be termed the first "crime and punishment" story. It begins with the command that God gives to the human beings not to eat the fruit, ascends to a climax with the transgression of the command, and then descends from the climax to the consequences of the transgression: the discovery, the trial and the punishment. In the conclusion, the man and woman are expelled from the garden. Genesis 3 is concerned with the question of human beings limited by sin, suffering and death. In other words, the narrative is concerned with human beings in their limited state. To aspire after life comes up against the inevitable barrier of death. In fact, if we read Gen 3:22 carefully, we can see that according to this most ancient thoughtful writer, immortality belongs only to God.

²² Then the LORD God said, "See, the man has become like one of us, knowing good and evil; and now, he might reach out his hand and take also from the tree of life, and eat, and live forever." ²³ Therefore the LORD God sent him forth from the garden of Eden, to till the ground from which he was taken. ²⁴ He drove out the man; and at the east of the garden of Eden he placed the cherubim, and a sword flaming and turning to guard the way to the tree of life.
(GENESIS 3:22–24)

This is not a story about a cruel God, but an early reflection on the mortality of humankind. We are not gods!

According to verses 3:17–18, the moral order bears a close relationship to the cosmic order: (Terence Fretheim, "Genesis", in *The New Interpreter's Bible*, ed. Leander E. Keck et al, Nashville, Abingdon Press, 1994, p369).

¹⁷ And to the man he said, "Because you have listened to the voice of your wife, and have eaten of the tree about which I commanded you," You shall not eat of it," cursed is the ground because of you; in toil you shall eat of it all the days of your life; ¹⁸ thorns and thistles it shall bring forth for you; and you shall eat the plants of the field.
(GENESIS 3:17–18)

This passage resonates with contemporary ears. While the curse on the ground seems quite unfair, it reflects the ancient wisdom that what human beings do affects not only themselves but also their surroundings. The choice of the woman and the man to transgress affects each other but it also has ill-effects upon the earth. Human sin has pervasive ill-effects upon all relationships and creation itself.

The narrative is permeated with the concept of relationship. The man is created because there was no-one to till the earth; God brings the animals to Adam to name them and to name someone was to enter into relationship with them; finally, the human-human relationship becomes paramount, second only to the human-divine relationship. When Adam exclaims:"This at last is bone of my bones and flesh of my flesh; this one shall be called Woman, for out of Man this one was taken," he is exulting in the knowledge that, at last, he has found a true companion. Certainly, in a gender-aware contemporary world, the idea of Woman being created from a man's rib does not sit well. But if we can transcend that challenge, we can see that the saying is an idiomatic one indicating relationship. For example, when Jacob meets Rachel, his cousin, for the first time, he is overwhelmed by emotion and Laban his uncle welcomes him into his house with the words, "Surely you are my bone and my flesh!"(Genesis 29:14) Adam recognises in the woman another human being as his true companion.

The Atrahasis epic with its primitive idea of gods is left behind, and develops into a narrative about human responsibility for sin. The flood narrative continues the "crime and punishment" theme but, in the end, redemption has the final word: "But God remembered Noah and all the wild animals and all the domestic animals that were with him in the ark. And God made a wind blow over the earth, and the waters subsided.(Gen 8:1) God "recreates" and pronounces the salvific words:

> As long as the earth endures,
> seedtime and harvest,
> cold and heat,
> summer and winter,
> day and night,
> shall not cease.
> (GENESIS 8:22)

THE ANCESTOR CYCLES

The patriarchal and matriarchal narratives of Genesis 12–37 are a collection of sagas and legends which relate Israel's developing understanding of its history as a people chosen by, and committed to, the one God, YHWH. The sagas circulated orally before being edited into a cycle of stories. The patriarchal narratives need to be read from a literary-critical and theological rather than a historical point of view. Biblical scholars who deal especially with the study of Form Criticism tell us that they are etiologies, that is, they are stories told to explain the origins of things.

GENESIS 6–9 THE FLOOD

Atrahasis Epic
- Creation of Human Race
- Problems with the Human Race
- Noise of multiplied human race bothers Enlil
- Enki is ordered to flood the earth
- Atrahasis is ordered to build a boat
- Earth is flooded
- Aftermath
- Gods suffer hunger and thirst when sacrifices cease

Outline Genesis 6–9
- 6:9–10 Introduction: Noah as a just man
- 6:11–12 Lawlessness in God's creation
- 6:13–22 First divine address: I will destroy
- 7:1–10 Second divine address: enter the ark
- 7:11–16 Beginning of the flood
- 7:17–23 Rising of the flood waters
- 7:24-8:14 Drying of the Earth
- 8:15-22 Sacrifices; God's resolve "never again"
- Chapter 9 Covenant and Blessing

DID YOU KNOW?

Indigenous Australians have many etiologies which they use to pass on to new generations the stories about how the Earth and its people came to be as they are.

The Story of the Covenant

¹⁹ God said, "No, but your wife Sarah shall bear you a son, and you shall name him Isaac. I will establish my covenant with him as an everlasting covenant for his offspring after him. ²⁰ As for Ishmael, I have heard you; I will bless him and make him fruitful and exceedingly numerous; he shall be the father of twelve princes, and I will make him a great nation. ²¹ But my covenant I will establish with Isaac, whom Sarah shall bear to you at this season next year."
(GENESIS 7:19–21)

The barrenness of Sarah, Abraham's wife, seems to prevent the promise of blessing being fulfilled. Gen 16 provides us with a story in which Sarah takes the initiative to solve the problem. She gives Hagar the Egyptian slave to Abraham as his wife, to provide offspring for him. Hagar's attitude to Sarah changes after she conceives. In the ancient world, women who could not bear children were often scorned. Abraham leaves the two wives to settle the matter between them and Sarah treats Hagar harshly. Hagar flees into the wilderness, thus putting her child's life and future at risk. God intervenes to help Hagar and the child. God promises Hagar: "I will so greatly multiply your offspring that they cannot be counted for multitude (Genesis 16:10)". This is in fact the same promise that God gave to Abraham. Hagar names God "El-roi" (God sees) and she names her son Ishmael (God hears). This story provides a basis for a biblical account of Ishmael's descendants as the subjects of God's blessings. Ishmael is seen by Islamic peoples as their ancestor. The biblical account now focuses on Isaac and the story continues.

If you have ever been shocked by the Abraham-Isaac narrative, where God commands Abraham to sacrifice Isaac (Genesis 22:1–18), try to think of it as a narrative showing Abraham's faith. Abraham's faith, however, is shown not in placing his only son at God's sacrificial whim, but his absolute faith that God would give him descendants through Isaac as God promised in Genesis 17:19–20. If Abraham sacrifices Isaac, where would that leave God's promise? Abraham trusts in God's word and God's goodness.

The story of Isaac ends with the "etiological" explanation of the name of the place where Abraham prepared the sacrificial spot, "God will provide". In the Hebrew language in which the story was written, the sentence actually says, "God will see". There is a theme of "seeing" running through these chapters. The implication is that God will see what the people need and will provide for those needs. God does indeed provide the ram for the sacrifice. Abraham's trust in God's promise was well-founded. God did not want the sacrifice of Isaac. Indeed, some scholars look upon the narrative as showing the point where Israel broke with surrounding cultures in the practice of child sacrifice. Isaac was redeemed by the substitution of the ram.

Abraham and Isaac

The Book of Exodus

Exodus is the second book of the Old Testament. It is a story of liberation from oppression, but it is also a story of violence. Some contemporary readers find this difficult. They expect biblical stories to accord with our modern preference for peace. We must remember, however, that in the ancient world where war was an ever-present reality, people believed God should protect them against their enemies. Exodus is the story of a people rescued by a warrior God—a God who commits non-negotiably to the people who have been liberated. It is full of joy and grief, of certainties and ambiguities. It is the story of a people liberated from oppression as slaves in Egypt, but who constantly had to be reminded not to oppress others.

The first chapters of Exodus introduce us to Moses, whom God chooses to take the message to Pharaoh to let the Israelites go free (Exodus 4:23). Pharaoh, however, did not want to lose his forced labour, and it took the plagues to persuade him otherwise. The story of the plagues culminates in the terrible event of the death of the firstborn of the Egyptians. By the sign of the blood sprinkled on the doorposts of the Hebrews, the angel of death "passes over" their homes and spares the Hebrews from the same plague. This event is to be remembered forever in a festival, now called the Passover. Jewish people to this day celebrate the Passover, or the *pesach*. The text of Exodus 12:14–28, which gives directions on how the festival is to be celebrated, is full of references to "remembering". To remember, in biblical thought, means to think of something through action. It re-creates a past event, as it were, and brings it into the present.

If you have ever been used to reciting the Ten Commandments you may recall that the text begins: "I am the Lord your God who brought you out of the land of Egypt, out of the house of bondage. You shall have no gods before me" (Exodus 20:2). After the crossing of the Sea—when God finally rescues the Israelites from the pursuing Egyptians—God gives the people the Law to follow, as a sign of the Covenant made between God and the people. The story of the liberation recounted in Exodus is thus remembered in the hearts of the people, in their festival of the Passover and their Law. But the remembering must also take the form of moral behaviours. In the Book of Deuteronomy—the final book of the Pentateuch—the people are commanded to remember their own plight as slaves in Egypt, their rescue by the God of Liberation, and to ensure that they do not impose slavery on others. See, for example, these texts from the book of Deuteronomy:

> [13] Six days you shall labour and do all your work. [14] But the seventh day is a sabbath to the LORD your God; you shall not do any work—you, or your son or your daughter, or your male or female slave, or your ox or your donkey, or any of your livestock, or the resident alien in your towns, so that your male and female slave may rest as well as you. [15] Remember that you were a slave in the land of Egypt, and the LORD your God brought you out from there with a mighty hand and an outstretched arm; therefore the LORD your God commanded you to keep the sabbath day.
> (DEUTEROMONY 5:133–15)

This text bases the Sabbath, with its call to give priority to God, in the act of God's liberation of the people from oppression in Egypt. But this act of worship has an outreach into behaviour towards one's neighbour:

> [12] If a member of your community, whether a Hebrew man or a Hebrew woman, is sold to you and works for you six years, in the seventh year you shall set that person free. [13] And when you send a male slave out from you a free person, you shall not send him out empty-handed. [14] Provide liberally out of your flock, your threshing floor, and your wine press, thus giving to him some of the bounty with which the LORD your God has blessed you. [15] Remember that you were a slave in the land of Egypt, and the LORD your God redeemed you; for this reason I lay this command upon you today.
> (DEUTEROMONY 15:12–15)

> [19] When you reap your harvest in your field and forget a sheaf in the field, you shall not go back to get it; it shall be left for the alien, the orphan, and the widow, so that the LORD your God may bless you in all your undertakings. [20] When you beat your olive trees, do not strip what is left; it shall be for the alien, the orphan, and the widow. [21] When you gather the grapes of your vineyard, do not glean what is left; it shall be for the alien, the orphan, and the widow. [22] Remember that you were a slave in the land of Egypt; therefore I am commanding you to do this.
> (DEUTEROMONY 24:193–22)

In these texts the "remembering" becomes a moral motivation: because they were once slaves, they must not oppress others.

The Exodus can be seen as the saving event that forged the relationship between YHWH and the "chosen people".

The Book of Exodus reached its present form during the sixth-

century BCE exile in Babylonia, or soon after, with the final shaping of the Priestly tradition. The sixth century BCE was a watershed in Jewish history because, in 587 BCE, the Temple was destroyed and all the elite of Israel were removed from their homes and marched off to Babylon. Here they were faced with the question, "How can we sing the Lord's song in a strange land"? (Psalm 137) They had to find new ways of worshipping their God in the absence of the Temple. This was the time when circumcision, the Law, and the Passover and the other festivals became the identifying marks of "the Jews". The exilic or post-exilic community had to practise its faith in a foreign environment without the Temple cult. The book of Exodus is a literary, pastoral, liturgical and theological response to this crisis.

The liberation from the Egyptian pharaoh is remembered throughout Jewish history. During the Exile under the "Babylonian Pharaoh", Nebuchadnezzar, (Walter Brueggemann, "Exodus" in *The New Interpreter's Bible*, ed Leander Keck et al, Nashville, Abingdon Press, 1994, page 680) the story of freedom was remembered and recorded; in more recent history, its symbolism was employed by African-American slaves, and the theme of the Exodus is woven throughout the history of contemporary Jews and the establishment of the State of Israel.

The remainder of the book of Exodus, the book of Leviticus and much of the book of Numbers, contains legal material. When we first looked at the divisions of the Hebrew Bible we noted that in the Jewish division the first five books are called Torah or Law. Although there are large sections of narrative and story within the Torah, we also find large portions dedicated to law. The significance of this can only be fully understood in terms of Israel's understanding of itself as being in a covenant relationship with God. It is the law which helps to define the nature of the relationship and the obligations of the community in terms of living within a covenant relationship.

Did You Know?

This theme of remembering is present in Luke's Gospel (22:19) where Jesus commands the disciples at the Last Supper to "not-forget" him and to re-enact his actions as a "remembering" of him. We continue this practice in our Christian celebrations of the Eucharist.

THE HISTORICAL BOOKS AND THE PROPHETS

We have taken a very brief sojourn through the books of the Pentateuch or the Torah of the Jewish Bible. The second section of the TaNaK (the name Jewish people give to their Bible) is the Prophets. In the Hebrew Bible, these books comprise all the books from Joshua through to II Kings. The Hebrew Bible terminology is the Neviim (the "N" of the TaNaK, in English: "the Prophets") and divides the books into the Former and the Latter Prophets. The Christian Old Testament names them differently. The Christian Old Testament categorises these books as the Historical Books, which comprises Joshua through to II Kings, Ezra-Nehemiah and I and II Chronicles, and the Major and Minor Prophets. (See diagram on Page 6)

THE DEUTERONOMIC HISTORIANS

When we consider the block of material from the book of Deuteronomy through to the end of Kings, we must always keep in mind that a recording of history in the modern sense was not the concern of the ancient writers. The Old Testament must be read from a theological perspective. The Old Testament is deeply embedded in a people of faith and the writings of the Bible are recounted from the perspective of that faith.

Old Testament theology rests on two foundational beliefs: God had saved the Hebrews from slavery in Egypt, and there is only one God. (Deut 6:4) They perceived that the nature of God was essentially merciful and, as their God of the Covenant, deeply concerned for their welfare. They often strayed from that God, but embedded within their hearts and minds was their faith that they were created by God and anchored in God's promises through the Covenant. The historians of the Bible constantly urged the people to worship only one God, YHWH, but they often required reminding! The people may have worshipped other gods, but not the biblical writers. It was their task to call the people back to YHWH.

Biblical scholars detect a theological-historical hand at work uniting the books of Joshua right through to II Kings with a common theme. This theme seeks to explain why God could allow the Covenanted people to lose their homeland and their Temple and be taken into exile in Babylon. The theology of these books comes from a group of writers known to biblical scholars as the Deuteronomic historians. They are named in this way because they based their theology on the Book of Deuteronomy, which can be summarised as:

- One God, YHWH
- One people of the Covenant
- One sanctuary, and that sanctuary in Jerusalem

It is believed these historians wrote their first version of their "Deuteronomistic History" in the seventh century BCE, around the time of King Josiah (ca. 640–609 BCE), and a later group of the same "school" updated it when they were in exile in Babylon.

The thrust of the Deuteronomistic history was two-fold:

- If the people would remain faithful to the Covenant with God, God would protect and bless them
- If they broke the Covenant, they would be cursed

The Old Testament was a world of blessings as well as curses. It is a concept alien to our modern ears and our theology, but we need to remember that we are dealing with an ancient and developing theology. The Deuteronomic point of view claimed that disaster had stemmed from the worship in the "high places" associated with Canaanite fertility cults. Only in the Jerusalem temple was worship to be carried out. Josiah's reforms of 2 Kings 23 refer to widespread worship of the Baals and Asherahs, the fertility gods and goddesses; archaeological inscriptions and figurines lend support to this situation of idol worship. Some of the practices had a long history in a land which depended upon the fertility of the land for its agricultural way of life. The prohibitions brought the people of Israel closer to the ideal of monotheism, but it was an ideal still in development.

Since you saw no form when the LORD spoke to you at Horeb out of the fire, take care and watch yourselves closely, so that you do not act CORRUPTLY by making an IDOL for yourselves, in the form of any figure — the likeness of MALE or FEMALE.

According to the Deuteronomic theology, Israel as a holy people expresses its fidelity to God in the *Shema:* "*Hear, O Israel, the Lord your God is one*" is the great prayer to be found in the book of Deuteronomy (6:4–9). The Passover, hitherto celebrated at home as a family festival, was now to be celebrated in Jerusalem; the centralization of the cult caused problems for people who lived far from Jerusalem, but provision was made for them. Sacrificial meat could be eaten within people's own towns, thus fulfilling, in an oblique way, the association of Temple and sacrifice.

According to the book of Deuteronomy, the people of Israel were chosen…

> [7] …not because you were more numerous than any other people that the LORD set his heart on you and chose you—for you were the fewest of all peoples.
> [8] It was because the LORD loved you and kept the oath that he swore to your ancestors, that the LORD has brought you out with a mighty hand, and redeemed you from the house of slavery, from the hand of Pharaoh king of Egypt.
> (DEUTEROMONY 7:7–8)

The Book of Deuteronomy encapsulates the message of the prophets to pursue justice. It sides with the disadvantaged classes, widows, parentless and the aliens. Contemporary theology terms this theology as "an option for the poor".

Plaque of Asherah

THE HISTORICAL BOOKS

In the first two historical books—Joshua and Judges—are the accounts of the conquest of the land of Canaan. Joshua is presented as the Moses-like leader, completing the work that Moses' death cut short. Joshua's crossing of the Jordan is narrated as though it was another crossing of the Sea of Reeds at the Exodus from Egypt. After overwhelming the local inhabitants of the land, the tribes following Joshua are given their portions of land. Theologically, the land is presented as a gift of God.

Historically, it is likely that the tribes settled amongst the Canaanites in the manner of ancient semi-nomads. Indeed, the Book of Judges hints at this more gradual settlement of the land. Where the book of Joshua is told almost as a chronological narrative, the book of Judges is structured around the theme of sin, punishment, prayer and forgiveness. The people turn away from God, oppression follows, the people cry out to God for help, and God sends a deliverer, a "judge", to deliver them from the oppressor. Some of the most well-known stories of the Old Testament are found here. Characters such as Samson and Delilah and Jephthah and his daughter appear in this book.

The judge seems to have been a charismatic military leader, a deliverer from an enemy of the people. They were not self-appointed, or appointed by the people, but were chosen by God for special situations; their "rule" was for a period of time and they were given a gift, or a charism, in order to function. Gender stereotypes are broken here with the appearance of a powerful judge, Deborah, (Judges 4 and 5) who functions in the generally male domain of battle. She is known as a prophet, and she is a political and military leader.

¹ The Israelites again did what was evil in the sight of the LORD, after Ëhud died. ² So the LORD sold them into the hand of King Jäbin of Cänaan, who reigned in Häzor; the commander of his army was Sisera, who lived in Harösheth-ha-goiim. ³ Then the Israelites cried out to the LORD for help; for he had nine hundred chariots of iron, and had oppressed the Israelites cruelly twenty years. ⁴ At that time Deborah, a prophetess, wife of Lappidoth, was judging Israel. ⁵ She used to sit under the palm of Deborah between Rämah and Bethel in the hill country of Ëphraim; and the Israelites came up to her for judgment. ⁶ She sent and summoned Barak son of Abinöam from Këdesh in Naphtalï, and said to him, "The LORD, the God of Israel, commands you, 'Go, take position at Mount Täbor, bringing ten thousand from the tribe of Naphtalï and the tribe of Zebülun. ⁷ I will draw out Sisera, the general of Jäbin's army, to meet you by the Wadi Kishon with his chariots and his troops; and I will give him into your hand.'" ⁸ Barak said to her, "If you will go with me, I will go; but if you will not go with me, I will not go." ⁹ And she said, "I will surely go with you; nevertheless, the road on which you are going will not lead to your glory, for the LORD will sell Sisera into the hand of a woman." Then Deborah got up and went with Barak to Këdesh. ¹⁰ Barak summoned Zebülun and Naphtalï to Këdesh; and ten thousand warriors went up behind him; and Deborah went up with him. (JUDGES 4:1–10)

In Judges, war is the punishment for sin. As one scholar points out: "If Israel would remain faithful to YHWH, it would not need a king or a judge to rescue it". (J. L.Wright, *Military Valor and Kingship. Writing and Reading War. Rhetoric, Gender and Ethics in Biblical and Modern Contexts.* Ed B. E. Kelle and F. R. Ames (Atlanta, Society of Biblical Literature, 2008, 33–56), p 52.) We must remember, however, that among the biblical writers, some are anti-monarchic, and some are pro-monarchic. Contemporary societies can surely relate to these various opinions!

An example of one anti-monarchic voice is this one from I Samuel 8:

¹ When Samuel became old, he made his sons judges over Israel. ² The name of his firstborn son was Jöel, and the name of his second, Abïjah; they were judges in Bëershëba. ³ Yet his sons did not follow in his ways, but turned aside after gain; they took bribes and perverted justice. ⁴ Then all the elders of Israel gathered together and came to Samuel at Rämah, ⁵ and said to him, "You are old and your sons do not follow in your ways; appoint for us, then, a king to govern us, like other nations." ⁶ But the thing displeased Samuel when they said, "Give us a king to govern us." Samuel prayed to the LORD, ⁷ and the LORD said to Samuel, "Listen to the voice of the people in all that they say to you; for they have not rejected you, but they have rejected me from being king over them. ⁸ Just as they have done to me, from the day I brought them up out of Egypt to this day, forsaking me and serving other gods, so also they are doing to you. ⁹ Now then, listen to their voice; only—you shall solemnly warn them, and show them the ways of the king who shall reign over them." ¹⁰ So Samuel reported all the words of the LORD to the people who were asking him for a king. ¹¹ He said, "These will be the ways of the king who will reign over you: he will take your sons and appoint them to his chariots and to be his horsemen, and to run before his chariots; ¹² and he will appoint for himself commanders of thousands and commanders of fifties, and some to plow his ground and to reap his harvest, and to make his implements of war and the equipment of his chariots. ¹³ He will take your daughters to be perfumers and cooks and bakers. ¹⁴ He will take the best of your fields and vineyards and olive orchards and give them to his courtiers. ¹⁵ He will take one-tenth of your grain and of your vineyards and give it to his officers and his courtiers. ¹⁶ He will take your male and female slaves, and the best of your cattle and donkeys, and put them to his work. ¹⁷ He will take one-tenth of your flocks, and you shall be his slaves. ¹⁸ And in that day you will cry out because of your king, whom you have chosen for yourselves; but the LORD will not answer you in that day." ¹⁹ But the people refused to listen to the voice of Samuel; they said, "No! but we are determined to have a king over us, ²⁰ so that we also may be like other nations, and that our king may govern us and go out before us and fight our battles." ²¹ When Samuel had heard all the words of the people, he repeated them in the ears of the LORD. ²² The LORD said to Samuel, "Listen to their voice and set a king over them." Samuel then said to the people of Israel, "Each of you return home." (I SAMUEL 8:1–22)

Notice how Samuel's speech focuses on the word "take" when he speaks of the king's actions towards them. Do you remember the word "subdue" in Genesis 1:28? The Hebrew word was a harsh-sounding one (*radah*, where the final "h" has the guttural "ch" sound that you hear in Scottish words). Well, the Hebrew word for "take" is similar. It is *laqah*, again with the guttural "ch" sound at the end. This writer did not like the monarchy. He preferred the prophets such as Samuel, who is here presented in a good light (unlike his sons!).

The Books of Samuel

The Books of Samuel contain some of the earliest extended pieces of Israelite historical writing. Having said this, the rule still holds that the interest of the historian lies in theology. The hand of the Deuteronomic historian is at work here, editing the books to explain why Israel came to be in exile. It is a long road from the history of David, beginning around the tenth century BCE, to the Babylonian exile in the sixth century BCE, but theological themes of fidelity/infidelity to God run through these books.

It is evident that there were ancient documents in existence in the courts of David and Solomon and these documents were taken over by theological editors, called "redactors", and formed into our present text. The Books of Kings refer to "the Annals of the Kings of Israel" and "the Annals of the Kings of Judah" (see I Kings 14–15). This tells us that there were other written documents to which we do not have direct access. This means that older sources have been systematically reworked to produce a continuous narrative of the origins of the monarchy in Israel. The Books of Samuel contain traditions about Samuel, Saul and David, which at one time were a collection of sagas and heroic tales which have been worked into a methodical and purposeful narrative by the biblical writer. This narrative skilfully moves the reader towards what scholars call the "Succession Narrative" (II Samuel 8–I Kings 2) which deals with Solomon, son of David by Bathsheba, as the successor to David's throne.

King David

The Monarchy: Administration

While theologically the monarchy is presented in I Samuel 8 as a rejection of God as king, historically speaking the truth was probably far more pragmatic. According to I Samuel 8:5, the people needed a leader like "the other nations" (that is, the Gentiles, which in this context means the nations other than Israel), to help them fight off enemies and protect their borders. As an institution, the monarchy required a complex administrative system to support it (see II Sam 8:15–18; 20:23–26). Writing was necessary for planning the Temple and Palace building projects and for instructing the royal children. Systems had to be set up to organize the payment and collection of taxes, there was conscription into the king's army and records had to be kept of property ownership and events involving the king (see II Kings 10:34; 12:20). Thus, the appointment of a king meant central government. Before the monarchy, tribes were held together by worship and clan interests. Now they were united as far as government was concerned, with a standing army that the king controlled, a legal system, and one ruler over the whole people, rather than tribal chiefs. King Omri was said to have two thousand chariots (although five hundred was a more likely figure). The human and natural resources needed to support armies were considerable.

Victories on the battlefield were viewed by the people as divine confirmation of the king's rule. The "other side of the coin", however, was that successful enemy attacks, famine, plagues and other catastrophes could be interpreted as punishment for the king's failure to live up to God's expectations. The earliest kings, Saul and David, were transitional figures in these developments (Saul 1010–1000 BCE; David 1000–961 BCE). In the tradition of ancient images of warriors, these two leaders displayed both military valour and special status with God.

⁶ As they were coming home, when David returned from killing the Philistine, the women came out of all the towns of Israel, singing and dancing,

to meet King Saul, with tambourines, with songs of joy, and with musical instruments. ⁷ And the women sang to one another as they made merry, "Saul has killed his thousands, and David his ten thousands." ⁸ Saul was very angry, for this saying displeased him. He said, "They have ascribed to David ten thousands, and to me they have ascribed thousands; what more can he have but the kingdom?" ⁹ So Saul eyed David from that day on.
(I SAMUEL 18:6–9)

The theological implication here is that David had found favour in God's eyes; this is confirmed in I Samuel 15, a quite poignant text, where God rejects Saul. Reading between the lines historically, however, it is clear that while Saul reigned, there was a rival to his throne in the person of David. Saul was something of a tragic hero; his suicide on Mt Gilboa, with his sons fighting beside him, ended the tragic story of the warrior hero who became king.

REIGN OF DAVID: EARLY DAYS

David's origins were as a shepherd boy in the vicinity of Bethlehem. According to the early accounts of his rise to power, he was gifted at an early age. He was known as a good musician, a valiant warrior and a shrewd speaker, able to call on diplomacy when it suited his aims. There are three accounts of his rise to power in I Sam 16:1–3,14–23 and 17:1–58. These are clearly disparate stories, collections about a beloved hero with legendary qualities, worked into the biblical narrative.

David was a complex character, regarded as an outlaw by Saul. For his part, David respected Saul as the "anointed" of the Lord. His exploits as a hero helped him to gain the love of Michal, Saul's daughter, and the love of Jonathan, Saul's son. In later years, Michal and David became estranged in their marriage and so they had no children. This would have united the families of Saul and David. It was under the kingship of David that Israel in the north and Judah in the south were united. This was the time of the United Kingdoms, but oppressive practices under David's son Solomon and his son Rehoboam led to the secession of the northern tribes.

David set Jerusalem up as his political, military and religious capital. David's palace was set on a hill overlooking the city and this section was known as the City of David. David may also have assumed the office of the priest of the Most High. David planned to build a temple, but that was left to his son, Solomon.

Thanks to David's action in bringing the ark to Jerusalem, it became the holy city (See 2 Sam 6). The ark had been the centre of Israelite worship during the desert wanderings. The ark was seen as the place of God's presence. It was the depository for the Decalogue Tablets and the Bread of the Presence. Its symbolism was similar to other Ancient Near East practices of depositing covenants and treaties at the feet of their patron gods.

King David and Young Solomon

According to the biblical accounts, Israel became one of the greatest countries between Egypt and Syria. Extra-biblical archaeological evidence to support this assessment does not appear to exist. David was a good administrator who built up a fairly large state (2 Sam 8:15–18), but true international fame seems to have only come to his kingdom during the reign of his son by Bathsheba: Solomon.

The "Succession Narrative", which runs from II Sam 9–20, and includes I Kings 1–2, reads like a historical novel. Its purpose is to demonstrate how Solomon acceded to the throne on the death of David, even though he was not the oldest son. Solomon was the son of Bathsheba, whose story is told in II Samuel 11–12. It is not a story which depicts David in a good light; in fact, David spends the rest of his days paying for what he does here. In modern terms, we might say the narrative shows David's family as a dysfunctional one. Yet David became exulted in later theology as the ideal king. It remains something of a puzzle, but the clue to understanding this theology of David, Solomon and the Temple is in II Samuel 7:1–16:

> ¹Now when the king was settled in his house, and the LORD had given him rest from all his enemies around him, ²the king said to the prophet Nathan, "See now, I am living in a house of cedar, but the ark of God stays in a tent." ³ Nathan said to the king, "Go, do all that you have in mind; for the LORD is with you." ⁴ But that same night the word of the LORD came to Nathan: ⁵ Go and tell my servant David: Thus says the LORD: Are you the one to build me a house to live in? ⁶ I have not lived in a house since the day I brought up the people of Israel from Egypt to this day, but I have been moving about in a tent and a tabernacle. ⁷ Wherever I have moved about among all the people of Israel, did I ever speak a word with any of the tribal leaders of Israel, whom I commanded to shepherd my people Israel, saying, "Why have you not built me a house of cedar?" ⁸ Now therefore thus you shall say to my servant David: Thus says the LORD of hosts: I took you from the pasture, from following the sheep to be prince over my people Israel; ⁹ and I have been with you wherever you went, and have cut off all your enemies from before you; and I will make for you a great name, like the name of the great ones of the earth. ¹⁰ And I will appoint a place for my people Israel and will plant them, so that they may live in their own place, and be disturbed no more; and evildoers shall afflict them no more, as formerly, ¹¹ from the time that I appointed judges over my people Israel; and I will give you rest from all your enemies. Moreover the LORD declares to you that the LORD will make you a house. ¹² When your days are fulfilled and you lie down with your ancestors, I will raise up your offspring after you, who shall come forth from your body, and I will establish his kingdom. ¹³ He shall build a house for my name, and I will establish the throne of his kingdom forever. ¹⁴ I will be a father to him, and he shall be a son to me. When he commits iniquity, I will punish him with a rod such as mortals use, with blows inflicted by human beings. ¹⁵ But I will not take my steadfast love from him, as I took it from Saul, whom I put away from before you. ¹⁶ Your house and your kingdom shall be made sure forever before me; your throne shall be established forever.
> (II SAMUEL 7:1–16)

Note the play on the word "house" in the text. Verses 1–7 are concerned with a house for YHWH, verses 8–29 are concerned with a house for David and Verse 13a is concerned with a house for YHWH built by David's son. God promises the Israelites land and rest; David is promised fame, rest, sleep with his ancestors, and a dynasty forever; David's son is promised an eternal dynasty, God's faithful love, and a father-son relationship. It is from this text and its theology of "son of David" that the naming of Jesus as "son of David" in the New Testament derives. For the early Christian communities and their writers, Jesus was seen to be the fulfilment of the hopes that the people of Israel had placed in the Davidic dynasty, which were dashed with the fall of the dynasty and the exile in Babylon.

The End of the Davidic Dynasty and Exile

The covenant between God and David's dynasty was to be an eternal one. It is easy to see, therefore, why the calamity of the Babylonian Exile and the Fall of the Temple and the dynasty occupied the mind and writings of the biblical historians. How could God let this happen?

In 597 BCE Jerusalem was captured by Nebuchadnezzar, the ruler of Babylonia. At first he was content to extract tribute, deport some of the inhabitants and leave behind a vassal king. Not content to exist under Babylonian rule, however, the people made an alliance with Egypt. As a consequence, in 587 BCE, Nebuchadnezzar besieged Jerusalem. The city was destroyed, the Temple fell and large scale deportations took place. The scattering of Jews from their

Did You Know?

Archaeological excavations at Hazor, Megiddo and Gezer uncovered city gates with city walls wide enough for dwellings, two palaces and public buildings dated to the time of Solomon. The archaeological findings tend to support biblical accounts but caution must be exercised when accepting these accounts. We must keep in mind that the writers were not recording history in the modern sense, but a theological history. Nevertheless, Solomon's reign was remarkable for its cultural and literary activity, its music and psalms, its intellectual, political and trade connections with Phoenicia and Egypt, and the practical wisdom of Solomon. However this period of Enlightenment was carried out often at the expense of the people. See for example, the subjects' request to lighten their burdens (I Kings 12:4), architectural projects carried out at expense of alienating his people and the contradiction between his own luxury and the hardship of his people.

homeland is known as the Diaspora (dispersion). In exile the Jews enjoyed relative freedom but they had lost the land, which was the sign of God's blessing on the people; the king, the representative of the people before God; the Temple, the place of God's presence; and trust in the idea of a God who would protect them against all enemies. Psalm 137 expresses their sense of loss and despair:

> [1] By the rivers of Babylon— there we sat down and there we wept when we remembered Zion. [2] On the willows there we hung up our harps. [3] For there our captors asked us for songs, and our tormentors asked for mirth, saying, "Sing us one of the songs of Zion!" [4] How could we sing the LORD's song in a foreign land?
> (PSALM 137)

When the Temple was no longer standing, how could they practise their cultic worship? How could they sing the Lord's song in a strange land? Judaism was formed by the answers to this question. ("Zion" was a word often used to mean "Jerusalem".)

The exile brought about a change in their faith. The prophets, such as Ezekiel and Deutero-Isaiah, led the people to discover a new way of living when the Temple worship was no longer possible. Now, circumcision, the Sabbath and meditation on the word of God became the chief ways of expressing their faith in a strange land. It was at this time that the creation narratives as we have them in Genesis were written down. The priests wrote down their collection of laws for the people to live by, and taught the people that their God had not been defeated by the Babylonian God Marduk, but was in fact the God of all creation. The prophets gave the people hope by teaching that their God was universal, a God in control of history. Their God had allowed them to be taken into exile because of their own actions, but that same God would also lead them back to their homeland.

Solomon's temple

THE PROPHETS

The task of Israel's prophets was to awaken the conscience of the people. Since this is not always a popular task, prophets were often involved in confrontation scenes. True prophets were called into the council of God, and spoke not their own words but God's word:

> ²¹ I did not send the prophets, yet they ran; I did not speak to them, yet they prophesied. ²² But if they had stood in my council, then they would have proclaimed my words to my people, and they would have turned them from their evil way, and from the evil of their doings.
> (JEREMIAH 23:21–22)

Prophetic speeches are very often introduced by an appeal to listen: "Hear the word of the Lord." The prophetic speeches take various forms. The Hymn of the Vineyard (Isaiah 5:1) uses romantic poetry to get the message of God's love across, but it is tragically romantic and has no happy ending. Prophecy sometimes uses the lamentation or dirge: see Amos 5:1, Jeremiah 9:10, Isaiah 23:1–14 and Isaiah 14:4–21. Prophets often use allegory, a poetic device where the prophet uses an image with a hidden meaning: see Ezekiel 16 and 23.

Often the prophets resisted their call from God. For example, the prophet Jonah tried to actually physically escape:

> ¹ Now the word of the LORD came to Jonah son of Amittaï, saying, ² "Go at once to Nineveh, that great city, and cry out against it; for their wickedness has come up before me." ³ But Jonah set out to flee to Tarshish from the presence of the LORD. He went down to Joppa and found a ship going to Tarshish; so he paid his fare and went on board, to go with them to Tarshish, away from the presence of the LORD.
> (JONAH 1:1–3)

Another prophet, Jeremiah, argued he is a young man and not equipped for his task:

> ⁴ Now the word of the LORD came to me saying, ⁵ "Before I formed you in the womb I knew you, and before you were born I consecrated you; I appointed you a prophet to the nations." ⁶ Then I said, "Ah, Lord GOD! Truly I do not know how to speak, for I am only a boy." ⁷ But the LORD said to me, "Do not say, I am only a boy; for you shall go to all to whom I send you, and you shall speak whatever I command you. ⁸ Do not be afraid of them, for I am with you to deliver you, says the LORD."
> (JEREMIAH 1:4–8)

There were different kinds of prophets. The spirit (*ruah*) of God fell upon some prophets who then became the instrument of the divine will. These "ecstatic prophets" went around in companies, delivering oracles when an inquirer sought a decision from God. Some belonged to guilds known as the "sons of prophets" and they lived in communities under the leadership of the chief prophet. Other prophets were more closely tied to the great religious sanctuaries such as Bethel or Jerusalem and they served in a joint ministry with the priests of the sanctuary. These "cultic prophets" were regarded as experts in prayer; they brought the people's petitions before YHWH and communicated God's answer. Some prophets could be found living outside the communities in an almost monastic lifestyle; John the Baptist of the New Testament may have been one of these. Like John the Baptist, some prophets were highly eccentric.

The writings of the prophets probably come from the "schools" or disciples of the prophets. They are collections of excerpts of what the prophets said.

The "Classical Age" of Prophecy was the eighth century BCE. Isaiah (First Isaiah) came from Jerusalem and expressed hopes concerning Zion; Amos (c. 785–745 BCE) looked for a king who would bring peace and righteousness. This language has been taken into the New Testament and applied to Jesus, especially during Christmas celebrations. Hosea, a younger contemporary of Amos, came from the farming world of the northern kingdom and was opposed to everything implied by kingship. On a superficial reading we might say he would have fitted in quite nicely with the Republican Movement in contemporary Australia. But the context of the times was quite different. For Amos, kingship meant oppression of the people. He was against anyone who oppressed the poor of society.

Micah spoke for the poor farmers suffering at the hands of landlords. His immortal words live on in our liturgies and hymns: "What does the LORD require of you but to do justice, and to love kindness, and to walk humbly with your God?(Micah 6:8) As a man of the country, Micah was outraged at the oppression suffered by the people of the villages at the hands of the elite of the cities of Samaria and Jerusalem. He attacked the socio-economic abuses of his day. Those who experienced the harsh words of Micah were the rich who oppressed the poor, rulers who oppressed their subjects, unjust judges and merchants who cheated their customers. Priests and false prophets often aided and abetted the rich against the poor at the same time as they offered assurance of God's presence and protection. For Micah, the coming ruler will be born not in the royal court of Jerusalem, but in Bethlehem, among the humble clans of Judah, where David got his start.

Micah lived during the reigns of Jotham, Ahaz and Hezekiah, between 742 and 687 BCE. He was writing in the last decade of the northern kingdom, Israel (730–722). His prophecies announced the fall of the capital of the north: Samaria. He was prophesying as the Assyrian armies of Tiglath-pileser III (who conquered Damascus in 732 and Samaria in 722) were on the doorstep of the south. But the south would not fall—at least for the time being.

Hosea, in the north, used the marriage metaphor to symbolise Israel's infidelity to the Covenant. Some of the images are disturbing for a modern reader because they call to mind the problem of domestic violence. Such texts need to be handled with sensitivity, and an awareness of the changes in our social, psychological and gender understandings.

The prophets Jeremiah, Ezekiel and Isaiah

The Prophets of the Exile

The southern kingdom of Judah lasted for another century and a quarter after the fall of Samaria in the north. This time the conquerors were the Babylonians. Historically speaking, the defeat of Judah came through political machination and the siege at the hands of Nebuchadnezzar's army. Theologically speaking, the exile was the judgment of God upon the covenant people who had broken with God. God's judgment upon Judah began, therefore, with the first deportation in 587 BCE and continued with the second in 587 BCE.

Jeremiah

Jeremiah, from the district of Jerusalem, was active before and during the siege of Jerusalem. Jeremiah tried to warn the people of the imminent danger using all sorts of eccentric means. Jeremiah's message was that, contrary to popular opinion, Judah and Jerusalem no longer lived in a state of favour with God. The situation was one of imminent disaster and the only hope of deliverance lay in repentance and conversion. His hope for the future was that YHWH would give the people a heart to know God. The Sinai covenant would not be replaced but would be renewed with a covenant in which God's will is placed within people and written on their hearts. The last we hear of Jeremiah is when he is taken by his followers to Egypt—against his will.

The growth of the book of Jeremiah was a long and complex process involving the work of several redactors or editors. It was begun in the exilic period and was still not finalised in the third century BCE.

The New Covenant (Jeremiah 31:33)—like the Old—would rest on the initiative and authority of God. It would be different from the Sinai Covenant of Moses, because the people did not uphold the Mosaic Covenant. The New Covenant would fulfil the original intention of the Sinai Covenant, which the people—not God—broke. The New Covenant would rest upon divine forgiveness and the personal response of the people.

Did You Know?

To the Persians, Judah was known as the Province Beyond the River. The people from there were known as the yehudim; it is from this term that we derive our word, Jew.

Ezekiel

The prophet Ezekiel went with the exiles to Babylon. During the first part of his ministry his message was one of warning. The people of Judah were gravely culpable and God was preparing to punish them through the siege and deportation. After the Fall of Jerusalem, however, Ezekiel's message changes and where Chapters 1–24 contain oracles of judgment, Chapters 25–48 of his book propose a variety of words of hope and support.

The famous "chariot vision" of Chapter One symbolised the ability of God to follow the people wherever they were. This vision symbolised a change in the conception of God from one who was confined to the Temple in Jerusalem to one whose domain was worldwide.

Isaiah

The book of Isaiah shows a similar shift in tone, but this time the chronology is spread over a much longer period. Biblical scholars generally divide the book into First, Second (or Deutero) and Third Isaiah (Chapters 1–39; 40–55; 56–66 respectively), they all belong to the same school, and an editor has bound them together in one book. Where First Isaiah, written in Jerusalem as the north is about to fall, is full of woes, Second Isaiah gives the message the people in exile had longed to hear: "Comfort, O comfort my people, says your God. Speak tenderly to Jerusalem, and cry to her that she has served her term, that her penalty is paid."(40:1–2)

By this time, the ruler in Babylon was Cyrus of Persia (modern day Iran). Cyrus is given approval in the book of Isaiah, because he was an enlightened ruler who allowed exiles to return to their homelands. Indeed, he allotted funding for the re-building of the Jerusalem Temple. From this time we can speak of the Jewish people and Judaism.

THE POETRY: PSALMS, WISDOM AND APOCALYPTIC

THE PSALMS

We are ignorant about the date of composition for most of the Psalms. The psalms are usually attributed to King David. Probably a good number were composed during the pre-exilic time of David and Solomon (10th century BCE) and some even earlier. It is clear, however, that many were written after the time of the exile. The collection we have in the Bible includes elaborations and rearrangements of prayers which circulated earlier and were adapted for use by the post-exilic community in their re-built Temple. The editing of the Psalms into the final form we have in the biblical Psalter took place in several stages, extending from about the fourth to the second century BCE.

Similar prayers have been found in Mesopotamian, Canaanite and Egyptian collections.

For centuries, biblical interpreters of the Psalms believed that the names which appear in the titles were the writers of the Psalms. Since in the first section of the book almost all the Psalms are prefixed with the Hebrew, *le-dawid* meaning, "to David", or, "belonging to David", it was usually assumed that David was also the author of most of the untitled Psalms. But with the emergence of critical scholarship in the nineteenth century CE, these assumptions were challenged

Statue of King David

and found to be unsound. It is now recognised that the Psalms are not the work of individuals in ancient Israel and Judea, but the liturgical materials used in ancient Israelite and Judean worship. The German scholar Gunkel observed many references in the Psalter to liturgical activities, e.g. singing, dancing, shouting, sacrifice, prayer, and references to places connected with worship, e.g. temple, house of the Lord, gates, courts. Since this discovery, scholars realised that the Psalter is thus the hymnbook or prayer book of the Second Temple (building finished 515 BCE) and perhaps the First Temple (which fell to the Babylonians in 587 BCE). It is no surprise, therefore, that we use them in our modern liturgies, since they have long been adaptable for community worship.

As John Bell says, "The reason for the abiding place of the Psalms in Christian worship, both public and private, is that they cover in theme and expression, the whole gamut of human experience." In the psalms we find joy, agony, questioning, despair and hope. Since the true meaning of the liturgy is "the work of the people of God", it is appropriate that these liturgical prayers should bring everything of the human experience before God. (See John L. Bell, *Psalms of patience, protest and praise*, Glasgow: Wild Goose Publications, The Iona Community, 1993)

Did You Know?

Psalms were not only used in liturgical contexts. They could be songs celebrating a victory in war. The Song of Moses, celebrating the victory at the Sea crossing in the exodus, is recounted in Exodus 15:1–21. This song was probably an extended version of Miriam's song which shows the women of the exodus singing and dancing to the timbrels (Exodus 15:20–21) since the women sang and danced after war victories. In this vein, Deborah's Song still exists in Chapter 5 of Judges. Hannah's song in 1 Samuel 2:1–10 celebrates the conception of her son, Samuel. Hannah's song is very similar to the Magnificat, Mary's song in Luke 1:46–55.

The Psalms take many forms. In the Hebrew Bible, the Psalms are divided into five groups, the divisions being indicated by doxologies (prayers which give glory to God). It may be that the fivefold arrangement is patterned after the five books of the Torah. The entire collection is known in Hebrew as *tehillim* (praises). The Septuagint Greek Translation refers to them as *psalmoi*, from which the English term "psalms" comes. All but thirty-four of the Psalms, the so-called "orphan psalms", have superscriptions. These superscriptions include references to literary forms, musical annotations and names associated either as patron or author of individual psalms. These superscriptions cannot be depended upon as being historically reliable: e.g. the superscription of Psalm 30, which is attributed to David, refers to the Temple which was built after David's reign.

Seventy-three of the one-hundred and fifty psalms are attributed to David. Some of the psalms are called Songs of Ascent because they provided devotional inspiration for those on their way to and from the annual pilgrimage to Jerusalem. Others are called Hallel Psalms, and were used in Temple liturgies. These contain the refrain, "Hallelujah", "Praise the Lord". (105–106, 111–112, 135, 146–150)

Psalms may also be assigned different categories. These are Hymns of Praise, Enthronement Psalms celebrating YHWH as king, Songs of Zion, Laments, Prayers of Thanksgiving and Trust, Royal Psalms, Liturgical Psalms, Wisdom Psalms and nine others which are considered by scholars to contain elements of some of the rest.

The psalms have long played a prominent role in the prayer and music life of the Christian Church. The early Christians drew upon the psalms as a rich resource for their theology. The psalms are quoted and alluded to in the Christian Scriptures more than any other book from the Hebrew Scriptures. In the New Testament, Jesus and the disciples are recorded as singing the psalm at the Last Supper (Mk 14:26/Mt 26:30).

Psalms have been used as a basis for music by the great classical composers, by religious cantors and in the contemporary music world by popular artists, e.g. the rock group U2 used to conclude their concerts with an adapted version of Psalm 40.

[1] I waited patiently for the LORD; he inclined to me and heard my cry. [2] He drew me up from the desolate pit, out of the miry bog, and set my feet upon a rock, making my steps secure. [3] He put a new song in my mouth, a song of praise to our God. Many will see and fear, and put their trust in the LORD. [4] Happy are those who make the LORD their trust, who do not turn to the proud, to those who go astray after false gods. [5] You have multiplied, O LORD my God, your wondrous deeds and your thoughts toward us; none can compare with you. Were I to proclaim and tell of them, they would be more than can be counted. [6] Sacrifice and offering you do not desire, but you have given me an open ear. Burnt offering and sin offering you have not required. [7] Then I said, "Here I am; in the scroll of the book it is written of me. [8] I delight to do your will, O my God; your law is within my heart." [9] I have told the glad news of deliverance in the great congregation; see, I have not restrained my lips, as you know, O LORD. [10] I have not hidden your saving help within my heart, I have spoken of your faithfulness and your salvation; I have not concealed your steadfast love and your faithfulness from the great congregation.

[11] Do not, O LORD, withhold your mercy from me; let your steadfast love and your faithfulness keep me safe forever. [12] For evils have encompassed me without number; my iniquities have overtaken me, until I cannot see; they are more than the hairs of my head, and my heart fails me. [13] Be pleased, O LORD, to deliver me; O LORD, make haste to help me.

¹⁴ Let all those be put to shame and confusion who seek to snatch away my life; let those be turned back and brought to dishonour who desire my hurt. ¹⁵ Let those be appalled because of their shame who say to me, "Aha, Aha!" ¹⁶ But may all who seek you rejoice and be glad in you; may those who love your salvation say continually, "Great is the LORD!" ¹⁷ As for me, I am poor and needy, but the Lord takes thought for me. You are my help and my deliverer; do not delay, O my God.
(PSALM 40)

One of the most famous of the psalms of Lament is Psalm 137, made famous by the American group Boney M. Boney M's version omits the final lines.

¹ By the rivers of Babylon—there we sat down and there we wept when we remembered Zion.
² On the willows there we hung up our harps.
³ For there our captors asked us for songs, and our tormentors asked for mirth, saying, "Sing us one of the songs of Zion!" ⁴ How could we sing the LORD's song in a foreign land?
⁵ If I forget you, O Jerusalem, let my right hand wither! ⁶ Let my tongue cling to the roof of my mouth, if I do not remember you, if I do not set Jerusalem above my highest joy.
⁷ Remember, O LORD, against the Edomites the day of Jerusalem's fall, how they said, "Tear it down! Tear it down! Down to its foundations!"

Martin Luther

⁸ O daughter Babylon, you devastator! Happy shall they be who pay you back what you have done to us! ⁹ Happy shall they be who take your little ones and dash them against the rock!
(PSALM 137)

The final verse is not included in modern adapted versions, but it serves as a reminder that everything, including anger and deep despair, were included in the psalms. This psalm was particularly appropriate to the African-Americans of an earlier era who were removed forcibly from their African homelands by the victims of the slave traders and landowners.

Martin Luther referred to the Psalter as the favourite book of all the saints (R.C. Hill, *The Scriptures Jesus Knew,* Newtown: EJ Dwyer: 1994, page 148) and thought it self-evident that each one of them found in it psalms appropriate to the circumstances in which they found themselves. The psalms are central to the Divine Office, the daily prayer of the Christian community. Pope Pius XII in his Apostolic Constitution on the Psalter wrote, "The Book of Psalms is like a garden which contains the fruits of all the other books, grows a crop of song and so adds its own special fruit to the rest." In the Middle Ages Palestrina (1525–1594) composed over 400 motets and settings for the psalms.

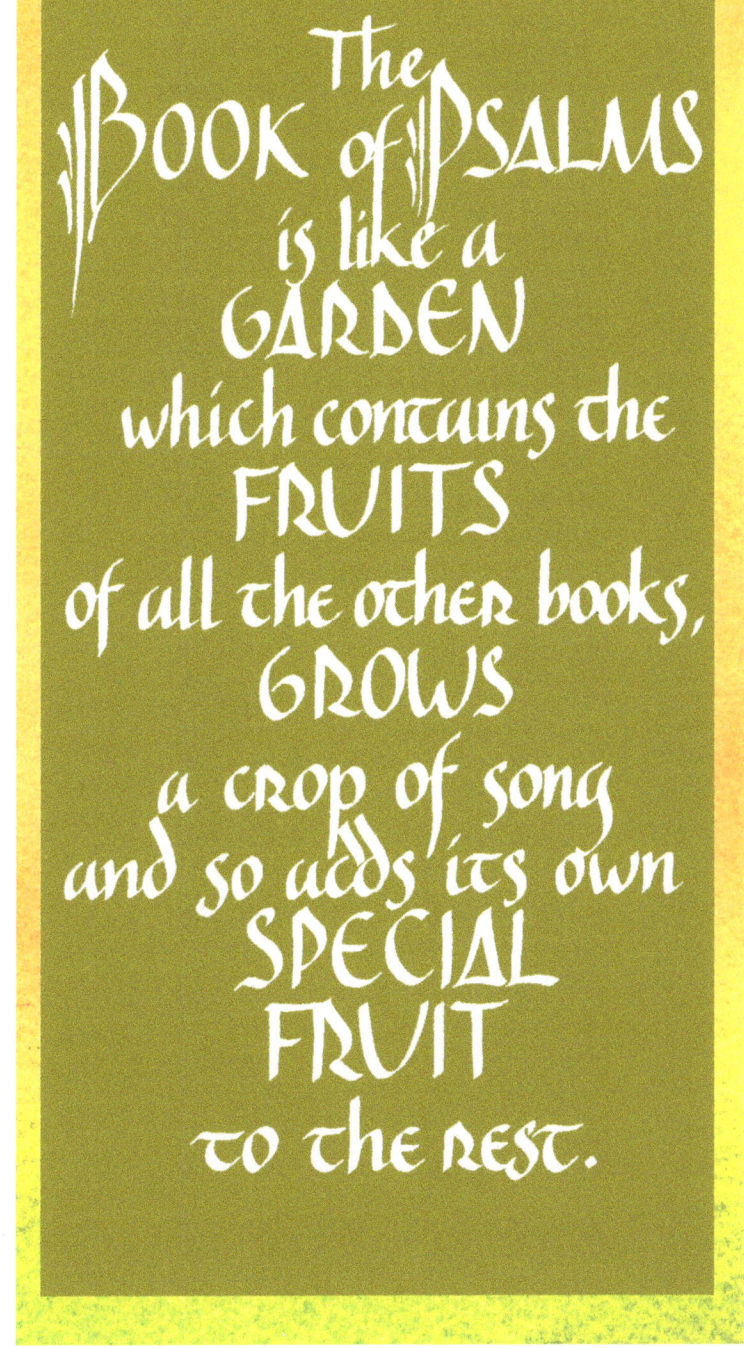

The Book of Psalms is like a Garden which contains the Fruits of all the other books, Grows a crop of song and so adds its own Special Fruit to the rest.

THE WISDOM BOOKS

WHAT IS WISDOM?

In relation to the Old Testament, the term "wisdom" is used for certain writings of the Bible, such as Proverbs, Ecclesiastes (Qoheleth), Job, and the Septuagint texts, Sirach (also known as Ben Sira and Ecclesiasticus) and the Wisdom of Solomon. One of the fascinating uses of the term "wisdom" refers to the figure of Sophia, who is God's wisdom personified. Sometimes this personification is simply a poetic, literary device, but at other times she takes on a deeper significance as a revelatory, feminine expression of the one God of Israel.

The wisdom writings share certain common characteristics and perspective. Some of the wisdom writings do not overtly appear religious. They deal with everyday issues of living in the world, but always with the Creator of that world understood. The separation of the sacred and the secular did not exist in antiquity in general, and in Israel in particular, where God influenced the whole of one's life. Every act had religious consequences and derived from an understanding of reality that was shaped by an awareness of one's place in a cosmos and a design controlled by God. In biblical thought, God created through bringing order out of chaos, or the great abyss of nothingness. Thus, it followed that if God was a God of order, everything in creation must be ordered appropriately. That meant that if human beings behave appropriately, then all would be well for them. This view included wealth and status as signs of God's pleasure. We can see this approach in many of the Proverbs.

However, reality did not bear this out. No less than contemporary thinking people, the people of the biblical world could see that good people often suffered and wicked people were often successful, by material standards. The answer to this problem of theodicy, as it is called in theological terms, is to be found in the great book of Job. Job is the completely righteous man on whom deep suffering falls. His friends argue the conventional wisdom view. They say that God is just, and therefore Job must have done something wrong or God would not have sent such suffering upon him. But Job stands his ground, insists he has done nothing wrong and therefore, if the conventional wisdom is correct, God must be unjust. The resolution is worked out in Chapters 38–41 where God addresses Job from the whirlwind. We do not find in these great chapters an easy answer to the problem of suffering, but the poetry and imagery of these chapters have provided food for thought for many generations of biblical thinkers.

^{1}Then the LORD answered Jöb out of the whirlwind: ^{2} "Who is this that darkens counsel by words without knowledge? ^{3} Gird up your loins like a man, I will question you, and you shall declare to me. ^{4} Where were you when I laid the foundation of the earth? Tell me, if you have understanding. ^{5} Who determined its measurements—surely you know! Or who stretched the line upon it? ^{6} On what were its bases sunk, or who laid its cornerstone ^{7} when the morning stars sang together and all the heavenly beings shouted for joy? ^{8} Or who shut in the sea with doors when it burst out from the womb?— ^{9} when I made the clouds its garment, and thick darkness its swaddling band, ^{10} and prescribed bounds for it, and set bars and doors, ^{11} and said, "Thus far shall you come, and no farther, and here shall your proud waves be stopped." (JOB 38:1–11)

The poem deals with issues of life and death, chaos and order, freedom and control, wisdom and folly, violence and nurturing. In the end, the God of creation sides with Job. Suffering is not sent by God because of any wrongdoing on the part of Job. The God of these chapters is not an easy God but, behind the poetry, we can detect an ancient thinker who pondered the beauties and the complexities of creation. This book is perhaps the highest point of the wisdom literature, because it presents in beautiful poetic form some of the most basic questions of the universal human condition. The wisdom literature consists of reflections searching for answers to secrets of life such as suffering, struggling with finitude and transience, and the quest for truth concealed in the natural world.

The Wisdom Woman

The wisdom woman has been at the forefront in studies by those who seek to reclaim a feminine image of God. There are five great biblical wisdom poems in which Wisdom is personified. These are Job Chapter 28, Proverbs Chapters 1, 8 (especially 8:22–31) and 9, the Wisdom of Solomon Chapters 6–9, Sirach (Ecclesiasticus) Chapter 24 and Baruch Chapter 3:9–4:4.

Wisdom is always presented as feminine. Sometimes this is simply a case of grammatical gender; the word for wisdom in Hebrew is *hokmah*, which has a feminine grammatical gender, or *Sophia* in Greek, again with feminine grammatical gender. But in the great poems mentioned above, the word "wisdom" is often personified as a woman. It is quite normal for poets to personify abstract qualities. You might recall Shakespeare's personification of Time in *Troilus and Cressida*:

Time hath, my lord, a wallet at his back,

Wherein he puts alms for Oblivion,

A great-siz'd monster of ingratitudes... (Act III, Scene iii)

The question we might ask then about the "wisdom woman" is whether she is a simple poetic personification of one of God's qualities

or whether she is a feminine representation of God, and therefore theologically significant. An example of wisdom as a simple literary personification can be seen in Proverbs 1:20–33:

[20] Wisdom cries out in the street; in the squares she raises her voice. [21] At the busiest corner she cries out; at the entrance of the city gates she speaks: [22] "How long, O simple ones, will you love being simple? How long will scoffers delight in their scoffing and fools hate knowledge? [23] Give heed to my reproof; I will pour out my thoughts to you; I will make my words known to you. [24] Because I have called and you refused, have stretched out my hand and no one heeded, [25] and because you have ignored all my counsel and would have none of my reproof, [26] I also will laugh at your calamity; I will mock when panic strikes you, [27] when panic strikes you like a storm, and your calamity comes like a whirlwind, when distress and anguish come upon you. [28] Then they will call upon me, but I will not answer; they will seek me diligently, but will not find me. [29] Because they hated knowledge and did not choose the fear of the LORD, [30] would have none of my counsel, and despised all my reproof, [31] therefore they shall eat the fruit of their way and be sated with their own devices. [32] For waywardness kills the simple, and the complacency of fools destroys them; [33] but those who listen to me will be secure and will live at ease, without dread of disaster."
(PROVERBS 1:20–33)

> She is more BEAUTIFUL than the SUN and excels every constellation of the STARS. Compared with the LIGHT she is found to be SUPERIOR, for it is succeeded by NIGHT, but against WISDOM evil does not prevail. She reaches mightily from one end of the earth to the other, and she orders all things well.

In 8:22–31, wisdom is again personified but here she moves out of the realm of ordinary human beings. She existed before the sea and the mountains, before the heavens and the sky:

> ²² The LORD created me at the beginning of his work, the first of his acts of long ago. ²³ Ages ago I was set up, at the first, before the beginning of the earth. ²⁴ When there were no depths I was brought forth, when there were no springs abounding with water. ²⁵ Before the mountains had been shaped, before the hills, I was brought forth— ²⁶ when he had not yet made earth and fields, or the world's first bits of soil. ²⁷ When he established the heavens, I was there, when he drew a circle on the face of the deep, ²⁸ when he made firm the skies above, when he established the fountains of the deep, ²⁹ when he assigned to the sea its limit, so that the waters might not transgress his command, when he marked out the foundations of the earth, ³⁰ then I was beside him, like a master worker; and I was daily his delight, rejoicing before him always, ³¹ rejoicing in his inhabited world and delighting in the human race.
> (PROVERBS 8:22–31)

This text will give you some idea of the figure of wisdom which many biblical scholars believe is a feminine image of Israel's God. Very often in the Old Testament we encounter images of God as a warrior-like God. This is understandable in books of the Bible dealing with the conquest of the land, or liberation from enemies. But the wisdom literature presents another face of God. It is a gentler more mysterious face. These verses from Proverbs present a beautiful scene at the dawn of creation. The figure who speaks does not identify herself but it is clear it is the voice of wisdom. There are many unsolved questions about the figure depicted in this poem. In line 30 the translation in the New Revised Standard Version of the Bible is the Hebrew word *amon* "master worker". Another translation is "master artisan" Either of these is a possible translation and they indicate the world of architecture as God is creating the world. It is a wonderful alternative picture to the Genesis account of creation. But another, just as valid, translation of the Hebrew word *amon* in line 30 is "child". The poem would then give us a delightful picture of a little child who joyfully dances beside God as the world in being created! It is no wonder that some of the early Church Fathers used this text from Proverbs to speak of Jesus as "the wisdom of God". They believed this text gave them the language and imagery to speak of the incarnate Son of God. This would not have been the idea of the Jewish writers of this text, and the figure of wisdom is almost always presented in feminine terms. But whatever the original author intended, this text provides us with a wonderful opportunity for reflection on the mysteries and the beauty of the Creator God. The biblical scholar Kathleen O'Connor says of the wisdom texts:

> She is a tree of life, and in her hands she holds life (Prov 3:16–18). Through her, kings reign, princes rule, and rulers decree what is just (Prov 8:15). She pours out her spirit on her followers and reveals her words to those who seek her (Prov 1:23). There are many indications that the Wisdom Woman is more than a symbol for the virtue of wisdom. She is herself God. She existed before the creation of the world, and participated in creation as a major artisan (Prov 8:30). She is a tree of life, and in her hand she holds life (Prov 3:16, 18). Through her, kings reign, princes rule, and rulers decree what is just (Prov 8:15). She pours out her spirit on her followers and reveals her words to those who seek her (Prov 1:23). These are divine prerogatives. (Kathleen O'Connor, "The Invitation of Wisdom Woman" in *The Bible Today*, (29:1) March 1991, 91)

Another text on Wisdom you may like to ponder is one from the deuterocanonical book, The Wisdom of Solomon:

> ²⁴ For wisdom is more mobile than any motion; because of her pureness she pervades and penetrates all things. ²⁵ For she is a breath of the power of God, and a pure emanation of the glory of the Almighty; therefore nothing defiled gains entrance into her. ²⁶ For she is a reflection of eternal light, a spotless mirror of the working of God, and an image of his goodness. ²⁷ Although she is but one, she can do all things, and while remaining in herself, she renews all things; in every generation she passes into holy souls and makes them friends of God, and prophets; ²⁸ for God loves nothing so much as the person who lives with wisdom. ²⁹ She is more beautiful than the sun, and excels every constellation of the stars. Compared with the light she is found to be superior, ³⁰ for it is succeeded by the night, but against wisdom evil does not prevail. ¹ She reaches mightily from one end of the earth to the other, and she orders all things well.
> (WISDOM 7:24–8:1)

Here again wisdom is shown to be the one who plays a role in creation. These wisdom texts remind us that the Genesis accounts of creation, while the most well-known, are not the only ones to draw upon when we are reflecting on the Creator God. How mysterious are the ways of God, and how rich is the Old Testament!

APOCALYPTIC WRITING

Daniel 7–12

The genre of apocalyptic writing had its heyday in 250 BCE–250 CE. According to the biblical scholar John J. Collins, apocalyptic writing is

'...a genre of revelatory literature with a narrative framework, in which a revelation is mediated by an other-worldly being to a human recipient, disclosing a transcendent reality which is both temporal, insofar as it envisages eschatological salvation, and spatial, insofar as it involves another supernatural world...'

(J. Collins, *Apocalypse: The Morphology of Genre* (Missoula, 1979), 9).

The word "Apocalypse" comes from a Greek word meaning "to reveal". When interpreting apocalyptic writing, the biblical reader should keep in mind the type of literary conventions or "rules" the writer was drawing upon. Apocalyptic writing appears to tell the future because it usually refers to a "revelation" which has been made to the writer and then written down and sealed until the present time when it is opened. This is one of the literary conventions of this type of writing. Other features of apocalyptic writing include God's intervention into history, where God will break into the present and save the faithful remnant; and symbolism, employing such literary features as numerology, animal imagery and colours, etc.

When reading parts of the Bible that we might call apocalyptic, there are some tips to help in our understanding. Stay with the symbolic world of the writer, do not presume a literal interpretation, keep the historical background in mind and recognise that the writer is offering a message of hope to addressees who are in dire straits. The more fundamentalist readers of the Bible do not take this feature of apocalyptic writing into account but they see this type of writing as a prophetic foretelling of the future. A good illustration of apocalyptic writing is to be found in the Book of Daniel Chapters 7–14. Part One of the book of Daniel (Chapters 1–6) contain six stories about Daniel and his friends in the court of the Babylonian King Nebuchadnezzar. Part Two (Chapters 7–12) contains the apocalyptic section, while Part Three is deutero-canonical.

Background to Chapters 7–12

(Apocalyptic Section)

In 332 BCE, Alexander the Great conquered Tyre, Samaria and Judea. The Jews of the Palestine-Syria area became part of the Greek and Eastern civilization known as Hellenism. After Alexander's death, his empire was split up among his generals, the Ptolemies (the Egyptian Greeks) and the Seleucids (the Syrian Greeks). Generally the Ptolemies were content to let their subject colonies attend to their own form of culture and religious worship, but the situation changed when Antiochus IV Epiphanes (175–164), the Seleucid ruler, came to power. His political agenda was a common culture, and that was Hellenism. This Hellenizing culture was embraced by the Jewish elite of Judea, who were mainly Sadducees. The High Priest Jason set about transforming Jerusalem into a Hellenistic city with a gymnasium and Greek games (I Macc 1). For those who did not willingly embrace his Hellenising agenda, Antiochus used force. Jews were forbidden to keep the Sabbath or to circumcise their children, under pain of death (see 1 Macc 1:54).

In 167 BCE, the "abomination of desolation" took place. A pagan altar was erected on the site of the most sacred Jewish Altar of Burnt Offering in the Temple, and swine were offered in sacrifice to Zeus (see Mark 13:14). This was abominable to the Jewish culture, since pigs were regarded in their Law as unclean. Rebellion broke out among devout Jews led by Judas Maccabeus. As a guerrilla general, Judas Maccabeus was very successful and on the Feast of Hanukkah, 25 December, 164 BCE, the altar in the Temple was re-consecrated and Temple worship restored. This Feast is celebrated annually as the Feast of Dedication or Hannukah. In John 10:22 we read that Jesus is in Jerusalem to celebrate the Feast.

The time of Antiochus Epiphanes was therefore a time of political, social and religious upheaval. The Books of Maccabees and the apocalyptic section of Daniel were produced in response to the terrible time of persecution under Antiochus. This is the background for Daniel's vision of the Beasts. Generally the vision is interpreted as referring to the four kingdoms which influenced the history of Israel, that is, Babylon (Lion with eagle's wings), Media (Bear), Persia (Leopard) and Greece (Leviathan). The Dragon's ten horns represent the ten successors of Alexander, and the little horn represents Antiochus Epiphanes. The kingdoms correspond to the gold, silver, bronze and iron.

¹³ As I watched in the night visions, I saw one like a son of Man coming with the clouds of heaven. And he came to the Ancient One and was presented before him. ¹⁴ To him was given dominion and glory and kingship, that all peoples, nations, and languages should serve him. His dominion is an everlasting dominion that shall not pass away, and his kingship is one that shall never be destroyed.
(DANIEL 7: 13–14)

⁹ As I watched, thrones were set in place, and an Ancient One took his throne, his clothing was white as snow, and the hair of his head like pure wool; his throne was fiery flames, and its wheels were burning fire. ¹⁰ A stream of fire issued and flowed out from his presence. A thousand thousands served him, and ten thousand times ten thousand stood attending him. The court sat in judgment, and the books were opened.
(DANIEL 7: 9–10)

It is interesting to compare this text with another piece of apocalyptic writing, this time from the New Testament:

⁷ Look! He is coming with the clouds; every eye will see him, even those who pierced him; and on his account all the tribes of the earth will wail. So it is to be. Amen. ⁸ "I am the Alpha and the Omega," says the Lord God, who is and who was and who is to come, the Almighty.
(REVELATION 1: 7–8)

Daniel in the lions den

¹² Then I turned to see whose voice it was that spoke to me, and on turning I saw seven golden lampstands, ¹³ and in the midst of the lampstands I saw one like the Son of Man, clothed with a long robe and with a golden sash across his chest. ¹⁴ His head and his hair were white as white wool, white as snow; his eyes were like a flame of fire, ¹⁵ his feet were like burnished bronze, refined as in a furnace, and his voice was like the sound of many waters. ¹⁶ In his right hand he held seven stars, and from his mouth came a sharp, two-edged sword, and his face was like the sun shining with full force.
(REVELATION 1: 12–16)

It is easy to see how the Book of Revelation has drawn upon the Son of Man imagery in Daniel 7:13–18. This section of Daniel has influenced the "Son of Man" sayings in the New Testament. Indeed, many scholars believe that when Jesus talks about the "son of man" coming on the clouds of heaven, he was thinking in terms of Daniel 7:13–18 to describe his own mission. We need to separate the context, however. In the Old Testament book of Daniel, it seems clear that Daniel 7:13–18 has in mind the faithful ones of Israel who believe that in spite of present suffering at the hands of Antiochus, they will be rescued and judgment will come upon the perpetrators of their sufferings. It is noteworthy too, that this section of Daniel sometimes gives rise to an image of God as an old man with a white (grey) beard! Yet if we know the symbolism, we can see quite clearly that "the ancient of days" refers to eternity. Thus God is not the one who grows increasingly old, but the one who is eternally young!

We have come to the end of our travels through the Old Testament. It has been a brief journey, but one which I hope will have enticed you to revisit some of the books we have encountered in more depth, and search out and explore other books which we have not managed to cover.

Perhaps by now you are becoming more familiar with this strange but exciting land we call the Old Testament. Its pages are dominated by a passionate God who had a heart set on a little band of desert wanderers, not because they were more numerous than any other people, but because they were the fewest of all peoples (Deut 7:7). Their task was to spread the message of God's love throughout the nations, and we owe our gratitude to the writers who gave us these ancient Scriptures in order to spread that word.

It is fitting that the eternal word of God is to be found in the Old Testament which, in spite of the name Christians give to it, has a message that never grows old. Indeed, as the sage Ben Sira reminds us (Ben Sira 9:10): "Do not abandon old friends, for new ones cannot equal them. A new friend is like new wine; when it has aged, you can drink it with pleasure".

May you have many days of pleasure with the Old Testament.

Glossary

Anthropomorphism A description of God as if God was a human being e.g. see Chapter 2 of Genesis where God, in the manner of a potter, forms Adam from the earth.

Apocalyptic A form of writing stemming from a context of persecution.
It depicts God as intervening in history to save those that have remained faithful, uses dramatic imagery and literary devices such as numerology, and is especially found in the Book of Daniel and the Book of Revelation.

Apocryphal To imply that writing is "secret" or not approved for public reading. It is used for material that is not recognised as canonical. Protestant traditions use the term to refer to books that other Christian traditions include, but they contest (see *Deutero-canonical*).

Asherahs and Baals Fertility gods of the Canaanite people. Fertility gods were seen as important in agricultural societies to guarantee the cycles of nature.

Canaan The early name for the land between Syria and Egypt where the Israelites settled.

Canon The authoritative list of books of the Bible.

Chaos/the Deep The "nothingness" out of which God brings order in the act of creation.

Charismatic Endowed with gifts by the holy spirit of God.

Decalogue The "Ten Words", i.e. the Ten Commandments.

Deutero-canonical Books of the Bible whose place in the canon is disputed by some Christian traditions, but accepted by others (sometimes also referred to as "The Second Canon").

Deuteronomic historians The editors of the Bible, especially the books of Joshua through to II Kings, who viewed the history of Israel from the perspective of the Book of Deuteronomy. According to the Deuteronomic historians, when the people kept the law according to the theology of Deuteronomy they were blessed; when they did not, they suffered.

Diaspora Jewish people living outside of Israel.

Eschatological Refers to the "end things": God's reign breaking into history.

Fundamentalist Refers to readers of the Bible who believe that the words of the Bible should be taken as literally as possible.

Hebrew Bible The Sacred Scriptures of the Jewish people.

Hellenism When Alexander the Great conquered much of the ancient world, he spread the Greek culture. When blended with a local culture, it is referred to as Hellenism (from the word for Greece, *Hellas*).

Hermeneutics Generally means "interpretation" (from the Greek messenger of the gods, Hermes), but more usually used by biblical scholars to refer to the contemporary relevance of a biblical text.

Marduk The chief god of the Babylonians.

Masoretic Text (or MT) The most common version of the Hebrew Bible which was produced by scholars known as the Masoretes in the seventh to tenth centuries CE. They added the "pointing" (vowel sounds) to the consonantal text.

Monotheism The belief in one God, as opposed to polytheism, which is the belief in more than one god.

Old Testament That section of the Christian Bible which Jews and Christians acknowledge as their Sacred Scriptures. Jewish people do not call it the Old Testament, since they do not recognise the New Testament as part of their Scriptures.

Passover/*pesach* Jewish Festival remembering that the angel "passed over" the houses of the Hebrews in Egypt, thus sparing their firstborn from death. *Pesach* is the Hebrew word for the festival.

Personification A literary device where an abstract attribute is depicted as a person, e.g. when we speak of Old Father Time. In the wisdom literature, wisdom is often personified as *Sophia*.

Psalter The biblical collection of Psalms.

Redactor An editor of texts of the Bible; more than a proof-reader, rather a theologian who adapts and organises parts of the Bible to make clear a theological theme or message.

Ruah The Hebrew word for spirit or wind or breath.

Sadducees A party or group within Judaism—the priestly aristocracy and their descendants or followers. They disappeared when the Second Temple fell to the Romans in 70 CE.

Sea of Reeds Scholars now believe that the translation of the words from Exodus as "the Red Sea"—through which the Israelites escaped from the Egyptians—was incorrect and was actually the Sea of Reeds, but it is not yet clear where this is located.

Septuagint The ancient Greek Translation of the Hebrew Old Testament. It includes other biblical books written originally in Greek, such as the Wisdom of Solomon.

Shema The great prayer of Israel expressing belief in the one God. *Shema* is the Hebrew word for "hear" and is recorded in Deuteronomy 6:4.

Sophia Wisdom personified, which is found in the great personification poems such as Proverbs 8:22–31 and the Wisdom of Solomon 7:22–8:1. It is the Greek word for wisdom.

TaNaK The Bible of the Jewish people: T is the first letter of *Torah* (the Law), N of the *Neviim* (the Prophets) and K of the *Kethuvim* (the Writings). These are the three categories in which the books are organised.

Temple The centre of worship in Jerusalem. The First Temple, built by Solomon, was destroyed by the Babylonians in 587 BCE. It was rebuilt when the exiles returned (Second Temple), expanded by King Herod, but then destroyed by the Romans in 70 CE and has never been rebuilt.

Torah The Law of the Jewish people, which can also refer to their whole way of life and teaching.

Transcendence When speaking of God, this refers to God as distant from the material world, in contrast with immanence where God is seen to be more involved with humanity and the world. Because of the nature of God, the terms are not mutually exclusive.

Vorlage An original word or document, used as a source for later documents. It is not necessarily available to us, but can be presumed to have existed.

YHWH The sacred, unpronounceable name for God, revealed to Moses in Exodus 3:14 and can be translated as "I Am Who I Am" or "I Will Be Who I Will Be". The four letters are called the Tetragrammaton. Contemporary Hebrew texts write the letters with the vowels for Lord (Adonai) and thus readers can substitute Adonai for YHWH.